Rethinking Economic and Monetary Union in Europe

In the wake of the Greek crisis, the future of the EU is the subject of a great deal of debate. This book critically evaluates the current new monetarist model of Economic and Monetary Union in Europe, presenting an alternative post-Keynesian (progressive) model, aimed at addressing the current problems of trade imbalance and asymmetric macroeconomic policy infrastructure that are augmenting tensions within the Eurozone.

The book's approach is based upon the development of a common, rather than a single, currency approach, and utilises post-Keynesian policy solutions in order to create a form of EMU which will promote full employment rather than austerity.

Philip B. Whyman is Professor of Economics at the University of Central Lancashire, UK.

Routledge Studies in the European Economy

For a full list of titles in this series, please visit www.routledge.com/series/SE0431

Rethinking Economic and Monetary Union in Europe

A Post-Keynesian Alternative

Philip B. Whyman

LONDON AND NEW YORK

First published 2018
by Routledge
2 Park Square, Milton Park, Abingdon, Oxon OX14 4RN

and by Routledge
52 Vanderbilt Avenue, New York, NY 10017

First issued in paperback 2020

Routledge is an imprint of the Taylor & Francis Group, an informa business

British Library Cataloguing-in-Publication Data
A catalogue record for this book is available from the British Library

Library of Congress Cataloging-in-Publication Data
A catalog record for this book has been requested

ISBN 13: 978-0-367-66722-1 (pbk)
ISBN 13: 978-1-138-20334-1 (hbk)

Typeset in Bembo
by Apex CoVantage, LLC

To those European citizens who have viewed the way that Europe's current economic approach operates and who have thought that there must be a better way to manage our economic affairs than this. . . .

The good news is – there is!

Contents

Figures

Preface

The past decade has not shown Europe at its best. The sluggish reaction to the global financial crisis by European policymakers led directly to the resulting Eurozone crisis followed by the best part of a decade of lost growth, lost jobs and, for many European citizens, lost hope. The eventual response to these events was, first, to misunderstand the nature of the problem and treat the symptom (fiscal imbalances) as the disease (trade imbalances caused by EMU [Economic and Monetary Union] itself). Then second, to impose austerity-led deflation upon a continent struggling to recover from a severe external shock. Not surprisingly, this bitter medicine came close to killing the patient. Expenditure cuts to social policies were treated as a means of re-establishing international competitiveness, in an exercise of beggar thy neighbour deflating to the bottom. Demonstrations and even rioting in many major European capitals was the inevitable result.

Nor was the means of implementing this mistaken economic policy cocktail any improvement. The formation of an unelected 'troika' which imposed 'discipline' upon other Eurozone member states was perhaps an understandable reaction from politicians and policymakers used to operating at an elite level, but it was in conflict with ideals of democratic accountability and must have been difficult for those affected citizens to accept. This was particularly the case for Greece who, in the face of effective insolvency, was required to accept yet more debt in order to bail out European banks who would otherwise have found their previous lack of judgement in advancing loans without properly checking the ability to pay rather disastrous.

Observing from the outside, it was both pleasantly surprising and heartening that the Greek people reacted in such a positive and progressive manner to their difficult position. To have the courage to vote not once but twice for an end to austerity and to call for Europe to search for a new approach to manage its economic affairs was impressive, only for this brave stance to crumble under the pressure exerted by the 'troika' and financial markets.

It is no wonder that public opinion has registered a significant decline in satisfaction with the institutions of the EU and its leadership over this time period. No wonder too that another nation, already inclined to scepticism with regards to the power that the EU institutions have over ordinary citizens, chose this time to vote to withdraw from the EU. This has truly not been Europe's finest hour.

And yet, this is not to say that Europe won't start to recover economically – it will. Indeed, it has already returned to growth and, whilst it currently seems unlikely that this will be of sufficient rapidity that it will recover all of the lost productive potential from the stagnation of the past decade, even this partial recovery will improve matters for many European citizens.

Yet, this return to growth should not obfuscate the fact that the current single currency framework contains a number of fundamental weaknesses which have not been resolved. Indeed, it is the argument made by this book that they *cannot* be adequately resolved within the current neo-liberal model of EMU. That is the bad news.

The good news is that there are other alternative forms of EMU that would still deliver the momentum towards closer and deeper economic integration that the advocates of the single currency favour, but they would do so more effectively and at lower human cost.

The particular model of EMU that forms the basis of this book is derived from an approach advocated by John Maynard Keynes in the dark days of the Second World War, in seeking to design a framework that would enable economies to trade more closely together without this leading to systemic imbalances resulting in deflation, economic stagnation and unemployment. It would seem, to this author, to be a match made in heaven for the challenges faced by the Eurozone economies and the weaknesses so self-evident in the current model of EMU.

The intention of this book is to contribute to what I hope will become an active debate across Europe, to find a better way of achieving common goals. Observation of the Greek crisis, and the attempts to resist troika-imposed austerity measures, made it abundantly clear that popular opposition to the new monetarist model requires a clearer understanding of other alternatives if the status quo can be successfully challenged. It is not sufficient simply to voice opposition without a viable substitute at hand. It is my hope and intention that the ideas drawn together in this book will provide one such alternative model of EMU that would avoid most of the pitfalls of the current system. Or, at the very least, to stimulate consideration of other, possibly more imaginative options.

Acknowledgements

There are a large number of people I wish to thank for their assistance, directly or indirectly, in the preparation of this book.

First, I must thank my family and friends for their forbearance during the endless sunny days locked in my study. In particular, I would like to thank Claire for her patience throughout the completion of this project.

I thank Emily Kindleysides, Eleanor Best, Anna Cuthbert and colleagues at Routledge for their patience during the almost inevitable over-runs. I hope you are pleased with the final product, and agree that it was worth the wait?

My appreciation goes to my employer, the Lancashire School of Business and Enterprise (University of Central Lancashire), for supporting this project through freeing sufficient time for me to be able to complete the manuscript, despite the myriad of competing demands upon research time.

Thanks also go to the various colleagues and oft collaborators who have offered their feedback on the ideas contained within this book, particularly in their embryonic stage. Furthermore, I offer my thanks for the comments made by two anonymous referees on the initial book proposal – many of which were extremely insightful and have improved the text that you see before you.

Despite the help and assistance freely given by all those individuals named, as always, all errors that remain within the text are entirely mine.

I hope I have repaid all your kindness with a work that you will enjoy, and which will, in some small way, contribute towards a saner political economy in the future.

Philip B. Whyman.
Nether Edge, Sheffield.

Abbreviations and occasional glossary

AD	aggregate demand
AS	aggregate supply
bancor	bank currency – the form of international bank money which Keynes proposed as the basis for the ICU.
CFA	Central Financial Agency – proposal made by Arestis and Sawyer, for stabilising financial markets and the economy as a whole, through the use of macroprudential and microprudential policies.
ECB	European Central Bank
EFTS	European Federal Transfer Scheme – an automatic stabilisation scheme intended to target federal fiscal expenditures to those member states experiencing a disproportionately negative external shock in order to reduce asymmetric economic developments creating strains within EMU.
EMU	Economic and Monetary Union
ESM	European Social Model – otherwise described as 'social Europe' or the social dimension (*espace social européen*).
ETUC	European Trade Union Confederation
EU	European Union
Euro-bancor	the form of international bank money which this book proposes as the basis for a Keynesian (ICU) version of EMU.
GDP	gross domestic product
HICP	Harmonised Index of Consumer Prices
HOL	House of Lords
ICU	International Currency Union – a model developed by John Maynard Keynes in 1942, to solve problems of managing an international payments system that would facilitate full employment and economic growth amongst participating nations, and not tend towards persistent deflationary episodes. Keynes designed the ICU for global use, whereas his model has been adapted as the basis for a Keynesian model of EMU in this book.
ICU-lite	a variant of the full ICU model which could be introduced without the necessity of replacing the existing single currency

	approach. This would be more effective than the current neo-liberal model of EMU, but less so than adopting the full ICU proposals.
IMF	International Monetary Fund
K-ECB	Keynesian version of the ECB – proposed, in this book, to manage the ICU.
Keynes Plan	the 1942 ICU proposals.
M3	this is one measure of the money supply that is available for use in the economy at any one time. It measures narrow money (i.e. notes and coins in circulation and in bank deposits), bank reserves and securities up to two years. M3 and other measures of the money supply form an essential feature of monetarist economic policy as this approach links the money supply to inflation, and hence seeks to control the latter through control of the former.
MCC	Maastricht convergence criteria – conditions established by the Maastricht Treaty for applicant member states to achieve prior to acceptance into the single currency, intended to ensure prior convergence.
NAIRU	non-accelerating inflation rate of unemployment – a supply-determined theory of unemployment that proposes to identify that rate of unemployment at which inflation remains constant.
NMS	new member states
OCA	Optimum Currency Area – economic theory utilised to indicate the factors most relevant to securing a stable and viable EMU, and hence arguably should form the basis for assessing the suitability of potential applicants.
OECD	Organisation for Economic Co-operation and Development
SDR	Special Drawing Rights – a supplementary international reserve asset created and managed by the IMF. SDRs are not a currency but rather represent claims upon currencies held by IMF member countries. They are not traded but allocated to countries by the IMF, in order to provide liquidity to the global economic system and supplement member nations' official reserves where necessary.
SGP	Stability and Growth Pact – places restrictions upon national budgetary deficits and public borrowing.
TARGET2	Trans-European Automated Real-Time Gross Settlement Express Transfer System – an existing clearing and settlement system, introduced into the Eurozone, which is intended to recycle idle balances.
TFEU	Treaty on the Functioning of the European Union – one of the two primary treaties of the EU, the TFEU establishes the scope of the EU's authority to legislate.

TSCG   Treaty on Stability, Coordination and Governance in the Economic and Monetary Union – established the fiscal compact reforms following the recent global financial and subsequent Eurozone crises.

UNCTAD   United Nations Conference on Trade and Development – operates as the principal organ of the United Nations General Assembly in dealing with trade, investment and development issues.

UNICE   Union of Industrial and Employers' Confederations of Europe – more latterly re-titled as BusinessEurope, a Brussels-based European business association that acts as a lobby group for enterprises within the EU and six non-EU countries. It typically acts as the counterpoint to the ETUC when social partners provide input into the EU pertinent to the development of new regulations.

Introduction

Economic and Monetary Union (EMU) was intended to deepen European integration through the creation of a Eurozone within which member states would share a common currency, and which was sustained by supranational institutions such as the European Central Bank (ECB). Economic integration was, in turn, anticipated to strengthen social and political relationships between participating nations and facilitate the development of a European Social Model (ESM), whereby greater commonality of labour regulation and social provision were to provide concrete benefits to European citizens.

Events over the past decade, however, have exposed the inadequacies of this dream. Slow growth within the Eurozone has been exacerbated by its response to the financial crisis and the resultant Great Recession. Moreover, the logic inherent within the specific new monetarist model of EMU implemented by the EU has caused a misdiagnosis of the causes of the Eurozone crisis, with focus placed upon fiscal profligacy rather than trade imbalances magnified by the design of the Eurozone itself. In essence, the current approach to EMU is "broken" and the cost inherent in not overhauling the whole approach is likely to be "enormous" (Stiglitz, 2016: xx).

Unfortunately, thus far, the leadership in Europe have not proved up to the task. Instead, the resultant policy response to the fragility of the Eurozone framework imposed stricter restrictions upon the ability of participating nations to manage their own economies, whilst broadening the reach of supranational mandate into areas of pension reform, wage bargaining institutions and the privatisation of commonly held assets (Zezza, 2012). For those economies, such as Ireland and Portugal, who have undergone this particular medicine, the resultant reforms have been painful, whilst the social tensions within those nations remaining the focus of Eurozone scrutiny, Cyprus and particularly Greece, the medicine prescribed appears close to killing the patient.

It is no wonder that Krugman (2012: 447), when reflecting upon the experience of EMU in Europe, concludes that "it looks increasingly like the whole project was a mistake".

Yet, a quick review of the reactions of many commentators at the time that the existing model of EMU was first proposed, demonstrates that many of its later flaws were predicted well in advance of recent events. The neo-liberal model certainly did not emerge without considerable criticism being levelled at both the conception of EMU (e.g. Eichengreen, 1993; De Grauwe and Vanhaverbeke, 1993), the advisability of the particular approach chosen (e.g. Chick and Dow, 2012; Laski and Podkaminer, 2012), the operation of EMU institutions in practice (e.g. Feldstein, 1997; Boyer, 2013) and, most recently, the response of the Eurozone to the latest economic difficulties (e.g. Blankenburg et al., 2013; Baimbridge and Whyman, 2015).

Economists working within, and those deriving inspiration from, the Keynesian tradition, have provided a consistent counter-narrative to the new monetarist variant of EMU. Taken together, this body of work provides a coherent and comprehensive critique of the existing model of EMU, and the need for an alternative model to be developed and adopted, if the Eurozone, and perhaps the European project itself, is to prove durable in the medium term (Zezza, 2012: 52; Grahl and Teague, 2013: 677). Indeed, the *Cambridge Journal of Economics* highlighted this critical perspective in its May 2013 special edition.

Despite this, however, the neo-liberal approach was selected as the chosen model for the establishment of what became the Eurozone, which, if nothing else, indicates the strength of those opinion formers who adhere to this broad economic school(s) of thought. Moreover, it means that, with a few notable exceptions (e.g. Hein and Truger, 2012; Arestis and Sawyer, 2013), the quite understandable tendency has been to focus upon the advancement of piecemeal reforms which would improve the performance of EMU but would, crucially, leave the fundamental new monetarist framework largely intact in many of its essential features. However, whilst these improvements would certainly ease the pain for many within the current Eurozone arrangements, they would be a second best solution to its wholesale replacement by a Keynesian model of EMU, which would prioritise growth and full employment.

It is the conception and motivation of this book that the formation of a systematic, comprehensive alternative model is required in order to both further magnify the weaknesses of the current system whilst providing critics with a potential substitute model that would suffer from fewer of these flaws. Critics of the current system require a realistic alternative around which to focus their energies and, even if that is not precisely the Keynesian model outlined in this book, then hopefully this will provide the inspiration for others to develop a different approach which can solve many of the same issues but in a different way.

There should be no doubts that this would be a difficult task, not least because the entrenched neo-liberal hegemony and those whose interests it serves will oppose such change. Moreover, there will be many across Europe who are weary regarding continual change in EU rules and structures – what De Grauwe (2006: 728) describes as a general "integration fatigue" in Europe – and who would prefer to avoid yet another upheaval. However, concern about the political practicality of substantive change in the design and operation of EMU should not preclude the development of a viable alternative approach because, given the fundamental flaws in the current new monetarist model, continual underperformance will undermine the concept of deeper monetary and economic integration in Europe. If Stiglitz (2016: xxi) is correct, and "the European project is too important to be destroyed by the euro", then the current flawed neo-liberal model of EMU needs to be superseded by an approach that will deliver.

There is a timeliness concerning the development of a more progressive alternative model of EMU. First, in observing the Greek crisis, and the attempts to resist troika-imposed austerity measures, it became abundantly clear that the popular opposition to the new monetarist model requires a clearer understanding of how other forms of EMU might operate in order to develop a viable alternative to the status quo. Second, progressive political parties within the UK and elsewhere have found it difficult to elucidate support for a version of European solidarity which is at odds with the monetarist foundations of much contemporary EU economic thinking. For those who seek to realise this more progressive European project, new economic foundations need to be established which will reinforce, not undermine, these campaigning efforts. This book, therefore, seeks to make a contribution to the development of a viable alternative, within the Eurozone, through outlining the main features of a potential Keynesian approach to EMU. It is hoped that this may encourage a more fundamental debate within those groups who favour deeper integration but reject the inefficiency and austerity-bias of the current system.

There is a considerable body of work that those working in the (post) Keynesian tradition have developed over a number of years, and this book begins by drawing upon this material to develop a critical evaluation of the current new monetarist version of EMU. In the process, it establishes the fundamental flaws inherent within the current model that have directly resulted in its underperformance.

The distinctive feature of this book is that, rather than this critical analysis informing piecemeal reforms directed towards making the current model work a little better, the second chapter seeks to develop a systematic alternative model of EMU, based upon the development of a *common* not a *single* currency approach, and utilising post-Keynesian policy solutions to create a form of EMU which will promote full employment nor austerity. This alternative conception of EMU is based upon Keynes's International Currency Union (ICU) proposal, and which could provide the foundation for a progressive form of EMU dedicated towards high growth and full employment.

The remainder of the book seeks to build upon this alternative model of EMU by examining how monetary policy (Chapter 3), fiscal policy (Chapter 4) and the European Social Model (Chapter 5) could be re-engineered to support this version of EMU.

For monetary policy, this would go further than merely giving the ECB a new set of policy objectives to pursue, thereby broadening inflation with growth and full employment targets. The ECB would, itself, be redesigned in order to act as the supranational agency charged with the management of the ICU system as a whole. It will be reconstituted as the primary agency managing the ICU common currency approach, including the introduction of a new form of international bank money, the Euro-bancor, which will settle final international balances between participating member states. As the ICU would remain a closed system, the reformed ECB would co-ordinate national central bank control over foreign exchange and would oversee a more rigorous set of financial regulations and capital controls. The ECB would act as lender of last resort within the ICU zone and would utilise a set of both macro- and micro-prudential policies to pursue financial and economic stability, which would assist the ICU mechanism to seek to secure full employment and decent rates of economic growth as the primary macroeconomic objectives of EMU.

Fiscal policy would be released from the constraints imposed by the SGP (Stability and Growth Pact) and the fiscal compact, and a revitalised role for national fiscal policy would be created according to principles of functional finance. National fiscal policy would be designated to secure high growth and full employment rather than remain subservient to any arbitrary fiscal rules. Fiscal federalism may play a complementary role, through helping to stabilise EMU against the destabilisation caused by asymmetric shocks. However, the Euro-ICU model would itself assist in fulfilling both of these goals, as the system is designed specifically to maintain a sufficient level of aggregate demand to secure and sustain full employment, whilst the symmetrical rebalancing measures inherent within the Euro-ICU approach would assist in stabilising the common currency zone against the consequences of asymmetric external shocks.

Finally, the book would examine the potential for revitalising the European Social Model (ESM) within the Euro-ICU approach. Enhancing social protection and protecting welfare systems would appear increasingly incompatible with a monetarist version of EMU, where social costs and employment rights are viewed as constraints upon the maintenance of international competitiveness and a means of enforcing internal devaluation by Eurozone nations with a persistent trade deficit. However, within the Euro-ICU approach, both can be viewed as a means of supporting aggregate demand and of securing the required degree of social solidarity required to enforce the symmetrical rebalancing measures necessary to sustain full employment across the common currency zone.

Bibliography

Arestis, P. and Sawyer, M. (2013), *Economic and Monetary Union Macroeconomic Policies: Current Practices and Alternatives*, Palgrave, Basingstoke.

Baimbridge, M. and Whyman, P.B. (2015), *Crisis in the Eurozone: Causes, Dilemmas and Solutions*, Palgrave, Basingstoke.

Baker, D. (2010), *The Myth of Expansionary Fiscal Austerity*, Center for Economic and Policy Research, Washington, DC. Available via: http://cepr.net/documents/publications/austerity-myth-2010-10.pdf.

Blankenburg, S., King, L., Konzelmann S. and Wilkinson, F. (2013), 'Prospects for the Eurozone', *Cambridge Journal of Economics*, 37(3): 463–477.

Boyer, R. (2013), 'The Euro Crisis: Undetected by Conventional Economics, Favoured by Nationally Focused Polity', *Cambridge Journal of Economics*, 37(3): 533–569.

Broadbent, B. and Daly, K. (2010), 'Limiting the Fall-Out from Fiscal Adjustments', Goldman Sachs Global Economics Paper 195. Available via: http://www.irisheconomy.ie/GSGEP195.pdf.

Chick, V. and Dow, S.C. (2012), 'On Causes and Outcomes of the European Crisis: Ideas, Institutions and Reality', *Contributions to Political Economy*, 31(1): 51–66.

De Grauwe, P. (2006) 'What Have We Learnt about Monetary Union Since the Maastricht Treaty?', *Journal of Common Market Studies*, 44(4): 711–730.

De Grauwe, P. and Vanhaverbeke, W. (1993), 'Is Europe an Optimum Currency Area?', in Masson, P.R. and Taylor, M.P. (Eds.), *Policy Issues in the Operation of Currency Unions, Cambridge University Press*, Cambridge, 111–129.

Eichengreen, B. (1993), 'European Monetary Unification', *Journal of Economic Literature*, 31: 1321–1357.

Feldstein, M. (1997), 'The Political Economy of the European Economic and Monetary Union: Political Sources of an Economic Liability', *Journal of Economic Perspectives*, 11(4): 23–42.

Grahl, J. and Teague, P. (2013), 'Reconstructing the Eurozone: The Role of EU Social Policy', *Cambridge Journal of Economics*, 37(3): 677–692.

Hein, E. and Truger, A. (2012), 'Finance-Dominated Capitalism in Crisis: The Case for a Global Keynesian New Deal', *Journal of Post Keynesian Economics*, 35(2): 187–213.

Krugman, P. (2012), 'Revenge of the Optimum Currency Area', *NBER Macroeconomics Annual*, 27(1): 439–448. Available via: http://www.nber.org/chapters/c12759.pdf.

Laski, K. and Podkaminer, L. (2012), 'The Basic Paradigms of EU Economic Policy-making Need to be Changed', *Cambridge Journal of Economics*, 36(1): 253–270.

Stiglitz, J.E. (2016), *The Euro and its Threat to the Future of Europe*, Allen Lane, London.

Zezza, G. (2012), 'The Impact of Fiscal Austerity in the Eurozone', *Review of Keynesian Economics*, 1(1): 37–54.

1 Why is the current model of EMU not working?

The ideas of economists and political philosophers, both when they are right and when they are wrong, are more powerful than is commonly understood. Indeed the world is ruled by little else. Practical men, who believe themselves to be quite exempt from any intellectual influences, are usually the slaves of some defunct economists. Madmen in authority, who hear voices in the air, are distilling their frenzy from some academic scribbler of a few years back.

(Keynes, 1936: 383)

Germany's deep-seated macro policy folly – the country's notorious anti-Keynesianism – has brought Europe to its knees. Almost a decade into the euro crisis, Europe's common currency remains a ticking time bomb.

(Bibow, 2017: 31)

Introduction

The introduction of the single currency in Europe was predicted to have beneficial impacts upon growth and prosperity across the participating member states.[1] By creating price transparency, it would facilitate the further deepening of competition within the EU single market, whilst exchange-rate stability was considered to be a simulant to the further expansion of trade and, via the development of European financial markets, securing finance for new productive investment. Although the model of EMU selected had been criticised by a number of theorists in advance of its implementation, early evaluations of the initial years of the Eurozone concluded that none of these potential problems had materialised (HOL, 2007).

A decade later, and it is hard to find many commentators who sound as sanguine about the record of the single currency experiment. Indeed, the economic performance of the Eurozone as a whole has proven laggardly during the past decade (Mazier and Valdecantos, 2015: 93), whilst the operation of the single currency regime appears to have worsened the degree of business cycle volatility in the national economies of Eurozone members (De Grauwe, 2013: 6). To compound matters, the single currency area was adversely affected by the global financial and economic crisis of 2008, but, as other nations employed fiscal expansion and unconventional monetary measures such as quantitative easing, the rigidity of the macroeconomic institutional framework underpinning EMU was less effective at realising economic recovery. Thus, the Eurozone suffered a further downturn in 2012–2013, as can be seen in Figure 1.1. Indeed, by 2016 it had only narrowly exceeded the level of economic activity previously pertaining in 2007. Hence, Figure 1.2 indicates that its present slow recovery suggests that it will be problematic for the Eurozone to complete its recovery to

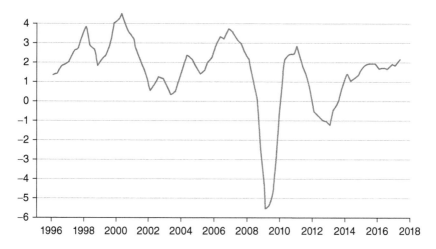

Figure 1.1 GDP in the Eurozone, 1996–2017

(Source: ECB statistical data warehouse, accessed on 6 September 2017, via: http://sdw.ecb.europa.eu/home.do?chart=t1.3).

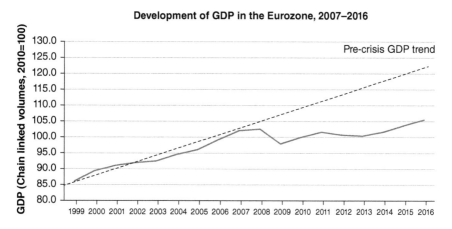

Figure 1.2 Development of GDP in the Eurozone, 1999–2016

(Source: Eurostat national accounts, main GDP aggregates, accessed on 10 August 2017, via: http://ec.europa.eu/eurostat/web/national-accounts/data/database).

pre-crisis growth rates and growth path, never mind exceeding them to recover lost productive potential (Hein, 2017: 61–62).

The free flow of capital, perceived by the architects of EMU to be one of the key drivers of future dynamism and economic growth, magnified the problems for the Eurozone. As Stiglitz (2016: 125–126) so eloquently explains:

> Ever-foolish capital markets thought the elimination of exchange-rate risk meant the elimination of all risk and rushed into the periphery countries. . . [then] . . . the same irrational money that had created the euro crisis, realising the enormous mistake that had been made, did what finance always does in such situations. It leaves.

The result is that Eurozone output will be permanently lower as a result of the financial crisis, and lower still because of the poor management of the crisis due to the constraints placed upon member states by the rules established to support the single currency (Stiglitz, 2016: 63). Moreover, in several participating nations, such as Spain, Finland, Portugal, Italy, Cyprus and especially Greece, the experience was much worse, with economic downturns for many deeper than during the Great Depression of the 1930s, and with GDP levels for all these nations still not recovering to levels a decade previously (Stiglitz, 2016: 67).

A gradual economic recovery cannot, however, obscure the fact that the Eurozone crisis highlighted a number of fundamental flaws inherent within the particular model of EMU chosen by the EU. These may be categorised within three broad classifications, namely:

1   Technical weaknesses
2   Design based upon neo-liberal or new monetarist foundations
3   Problems rectifying trade imbalances within a single currency.

Issues pertaining to the first of these categories indicate how inadequate technical design features have weakened the development of EMU, but which, by themselves, are not necessarily fatal to the eventual success of the project if adequate policy interventions and adjustments are undertaken. The second category identifies fundamental problems in the design and operation of the economic infrastructure established to sustain EMU. This is more serious, but a substantive redesign of these foundations could enhance the ability of the current single currency model to work more effectively. However, it is the third category where the current model of EMU is most fatally flawed and where an alternative common currency model of EMU would be superior. That, at least, is the thesis of this book.

Technical weaknesses with the current model of EMU

There are a number of technical reasons why the design and implementation of EMU in Europe has been faulty, and the single currency is a flawed currency area (Barba and De Vivo, 2013; Baimbridge et al., 2012: 96). The most obvious of which is that the introduction of European EMU was based on shaky intellectual foundations, as the convergence criteria (MCC), established by the Maastricht Treaty, focused upon transitory *cyclical* movements in *financial* indicators, rather than concentrating upon *structural* convergence in the real economy (Baimbridge et al., 1999). The creation of the single currency was, therefore, not based upon Optimum Currency Area (OCA) criteria (Mundell, 1961; Eichengreen, 1990, 1992, 1993; Weber, 1991; Bayoumi and Eichengreen, 1993; Baimbridge et al., 1999).

Rather than focusing upon convergence in real economy measures, such as the degree of factor mobility and both commodity market diversification and integration, the MCC rather narrowly focused upon similarities in interest and inflation rates, and limitations upon the ability of potential participants to run 'excessive' budget deficits and levels of national debt. The adoption of fiscal rules was intended to prevent moral hazard if individual member states were otherwise able to borrow excessively in the common currency, and thereby free riding on other members of the single currency if they subsequently got into financial difficulties which necessitated a bail out (Lane, 2012: 49). Yet even within the narrow conception of the MCC, the advent of the single currency was undermined by inadequate prior convergence between participating nations (Baimbridge et al., 1998: 5; Lavoie, 2015: 3), as political considerations to maximise participation dominated considerations of what factors economic theory suggested would constitute an 'optimal currency area' (Feldstein, 1997: 24–25).

The assumption was made that a shared currency would trigger sufficient structural changes to fulfil OCA conditions and thereby generate economic convergence (Boyer, 2013: 535). Thus, even if ex ante the establishment of the single currency, OCA criteria may not have been met, it is quite plausible that some or all of these same criteria may be satisfied ex post, through deliberate policy measures taken to increase factor mobility and through the natural reorientation of trade towards fellow participants in the single currency (Frankel, 1999: 30). However, it is equally possible that increased specialisation in production, encouraged by increased trade, may reduce the correlation of outcomes between participants in a single currency, thereby causing ex post failure to meet OCA criteria even if these same nations initially did so ex ante (Krugman, 1993: 260).

There is an expectation, amongst mainstream economists, that the operation of market forces will cause economies at different stages of development and at different levels of income and productivity to converge over time, as the mobility of capital and labour, in search of higher rewards, tends to equalise divergent performance of different economies. The operation of EMU would be expected to augment this tendency. However, set against this, market forces additionally generate cumulative causation (Myrdal, 1957; Kaldor, 1970) or centripetalism (Cowling, 1987). This is where an economically successful region or economy generates the profits that facilitate and attract additional investment, whilst a growing area tends to raise real wages, which in turn attracts an inward flow of migrant labour from less prosperous regions or economies. Expanding output will, in addition, potentially allow these regions to benefit from economies of scale, thereby further magnifying the initial competitive advantage of the area and thus exacerbating differences in performance (Kaldor, 1972). Less successful regions, by contrast, will experience lower levels of per capita income, higher levels of unemployment and greater constraints upon their ability to deliver faster growth rates to enable the process of catching-up with their more affluent neighbours (Arestis and Sawyer, 1998: 182). Economic growth, therefore, is path dependant (Kaldor, 1972: 1244).

Relaxing unrealistic neo-classical theoretical assumptions of equilibrium would lead to predictions of free trade increasing and not narrowing divergence between nations, since trade might enlarge differences in productivity between countries at different stages of development. As a result, Kaldor (1981: 593) concluded that:

> Under more realistic assumptions unrestricted trade is likely to lead to a loss of welfare to particular regions or countries and even to the world as a whole – that is to say that the world would be worse off under free trade than it could be under some system of regulated trade.

The evidence would tend to support the position adopted by Kaldor and Krugman, in that output crises would appear to occur more frequently for countries that have adopted the Euro (Bird and Mandilaras, 2012: 13). The introduction of monetary union has also coincided with increasing divergence amongst member states, together with a profound worsening of labour's share of national income of around 35 per cent over the last three decades (Zarotiadis and Gkagka, 2013: 546, 557–558). This should not be a surprise to policymakers since these fears were noted at the time of formation, and indeed, is one reason why convergence criteria were included in the basic membership criteria, albeit poorly formulated and weakly enforced (Weber, 1991; Bayoumi and Eichengreen, 1993).

An inadequate monetarist model of EMU

The current version of EMU, adopted by the European Union (EU), was founded upon principles drawn from what has been variously described as the 'Berlin-Washington consensus' (Skidelsky, 2005: 18; Fitoussi and Saraceno, 2013), the 'Brussels-Frankfurt Consensus' (Whyman et al., 2012: 8–15), the 'new monetarism' (Arestis et al., 2001: 115; Moss, 2005: 6) or 'ordoliberalism', which is a variant of neo-liberalism (Stockhammer, 2016: 367). In part, this model of EMU simply internalised many features of the 'German model', most prominently the prioritisation of price stability and aversion to debt, due in large part to the 'ghost of Weimar' and hyperinflation instability in the country preceding the rise of fascism in the 1930s (Dyson and Featherstone, 1999). Indeed, it was considered to be an advantage for those countries without prior 'sound money' credibility to have monetary discipline imposed upon them via the operation of EMU and a supranational central bank operating on similar lines to the Bundesbank (Smithin and Wolf, 1993: 376). However, the fact that the design of the current model of EMU was drawn from these schools of thought has created a set of fundamental weaknesses within the single currency itself, and its supportive framework.

The new monetarist or neo-liberal approach is founded upon certain basic assumptions. The first of these is that the economy has a tendency to move automatically towards its full employment equilibrium. This idea is often bound up with the supply-side determined non-accelerating inflation rate of unemployment (NAIRU), which is, itself, loosely derived from the adaptive expectations-augmented, vertical long-run Phillips Curve (Friedman, 1968; Phelps, 1968; Layard and Nickell, 1985). The NAIRU approach holds that the level of (un)employment is established by supply-side factors, whether these be the interaction of market forces and/or the balance of power in a distributional conflict between labour and capital. This is, in essence, rather similar to the neo-classical formulation that the intersection of supply and demand curves determines the long-run equilibrium 'natural rate' of unemployment, at a given real wage (Friedman, 1968: 8). This approach holds that supply-side factors are not influenced by changes in aggregate demand, beyond the short run, but rather are determined within the labour market. If economic actors possessed rational expectations and markets were perfectly competitive, it was suggested that active fiscal or macroeconomic policy would be harmful, either in the short or medium term, as it would result in higher inflation rather than expanding output and employment (Gordon, 1997). Indeed, under this set of assumptions about how the economy works, it would be *impossible* for governments to stabilise the economy (Backhouse, 2009: 21).

Inflation is viewed, according to this perspective, as a monetary phenomenon and monetary policy can be directed to its control, using either direct means (money supply) or indirect (interest rates) via inflation targeting. Central banks, independent of political influence, should pursue a policy of long-term, financial 'credibility', in order to avoid the time inconsistency problem, which is where the existence of imperfect information leads to governments being tempted to 'surprise' economic actors and secure temporarily higher employment by allowing higher inflation (Kyland and Prescott, 1977; Barro and Gordon, 1983).

One solution could involve the pre-commitment of the economic authorities to state publicly that they would not attempt to 'surprise' other economic actors with such behaviour and to either introduce a set of rules, which cannot be changed easily or establish an independent agency with the necessary credibility to pursue the agreed policy rules (Lucas, 1976; Barro and Gordon, 1983). This was additionally considered to have the effect of reducing risk premia imposed by international financial markets, since investors were likely to perceive a lower probability of unexpected inflation undermining asset values (Baker, 2000: 230).

In the context of the Eurozone, the European Central Bank (ECB) fulfils this function, independent of political control, through pursuing price stability as its primary objective and with only secondary concern about the general health of the European economy (EU, 2012). Thus, the economic infrastructure, imposed to support monetary and financial integration, constrains state intervention in favour of private-sector dominance to a greater extent than in other advanced economies (Blankenburg et al., 2013: 465–466).

The European employer's organisation, UNICE (Union of Industrial and Employers' Confederations of Europe), stated that one of the key advantages arising from EMU would be that it would impose downward pressure on wages and the social wage (Verdun, 1996: 76–77). Indeed, the Maastricht convergence criteria clearly operated as a trigger helping to overcome political resistance to welfare reform and undermining organised labour, thereby resulting in an increase in the share of national income absorbed by the owners of capital (Hemerijck and Ferrera, 2004: 260; Moss, 2005: 12).

The neo-liberal model of EMU is therefore theoretically consistent. However, it is also an inadequate model, as its theoretical basis is fundamentally flawed (Moss, 2005; Boyer, 2013: 535). For example, the rational expectations approach additionally assumes a market system whereby 'prices reflect instantaneously everything that is known today, and prices today reflect a consistent set of expectations about what prices will be *infinitely far into the future*' (Stiglitz, 2003: 152; emphasis in original). The policy conclusion reached is that government intervention is always inefficient and unnecessary. Yet, these conclusions, particularly relating to the supposed efficiency of markets, collapses if economic actors have differential access to information and/or have different beliefs, and there is an overwhelming weight of evidence to suggest this is the real position.

The problem for advocates of the rational expectations hypothesis is that uncertainty is not the same as risk. The latter can be calculated, on the basis of statistical calculation drawn from accumulated datasets, whereas uncertainty cannot be tamed by the use of probability calculations because the basis of this exercise simply does not exist (Keynes, 1936: 162–163). If the parameters of future events are volatile or unknown, then probability analysis is ineffective. Expectations of future events are influenced by the general state of confidence, the impact of speculation and instabilities due to 'animal spirits' or psychological aspects of human nature (Keynes, 1936: 148, 161–162). In an uncertain world, not even market fundamentals necessarily provide a reliable means of predicting future developments, since market valuations are subject to the impact of irrational herding effects and market volatility is exacerbated through investor irrational exuberance and/or panic (Alves et al., 1999: 207–208). Due to uncertainty, the presumption that markets will behave according to the precepts of the efficient market hypothesis is tenuous at best (Alves et al., 1999: 215). Therefore, Stiglitz (2003: 152) argues that "unfettered markets, rampant with conflicts of interest, can lead to inefficiency".

There is, additionally, considerable scepticism about the natural rate of unemployment hypothesis and the reliability of NAIRU estimations of unemployment equilibrium (Setterfield et al., 1992; Sawyer, 2003). The problems with this approach are such that it becomes of questionable value in determining economic policy (Galbraith, 1997: 102; Arestis and Sawyer, 2004: 33). Moreover, in contrast to theories of the supply-side determination of employment, there is considerable evidence that employment is determined in the product market by the aggregate demand for output (Rowthorn, 1995; Davidson, 1998; Alexiou and Pitelis, 2003). Indeed, there is a large and growing literature that claims that productive capacity has a large, statistically significant impact upon employment (Bean, 1989, 1994; Rowthorn, 1995, 1999; Arestis and Mariscal, 1997: 191; Alexiou and Pitelis, 2003: 628; Baddeley, 2003: 214). Consequently, both in its theoretical bias against active government policy, together with its bias in application, the equilibrium concept of unemployment causes policy to be constrained more than it need to be, with the consequence that unemployment is higher as a result (UNCTAD, 1995: 172).

A second reason why the natural rate of unemployment approach is a poor basis for policy design can be inferred from the theory of hysteresis, first developed by Phelps in 1972. This suggests that the equilibrium rate of unemployment is *path-dependent*, in that it depends upon the actual history or path of unemployment. Unemployment persistence can be considered to influence future unemployment rates because the skills held by an unemployed individual may deteriorate over time, as can their work discipline, confidence and hence employability in the eyes of the employer. The longer an individual remains unemployed, their search efforts may decline, together with their expectation that they may succeed in securing a new job. Hence, demand shocks lead to lower rates of capital accumulation, with initial impacts magnified due to the existence of hysteresis (Rowthorn, 1995). Thus, actual unemployment largely determines equilibrium unemployment, and therefore governments can shift the NAIRU by affecting actual unemployment (Blanchard and Summers, 1988; Ball, 1994).

Unfortunately, the EU's Lisbon strategy ignores the necessity for macroeconomic management. It, moreover, accepts the necessity of constrained fiscal policy as a means to dampen demand and reduce budget deficits and/or public debt, with the intention that this will in turn lower long-term interest rates and lessen the possibility of public spending crowding-out private-sector activity (Sapir et al., 2004: 51). As a result, the Lisbon approach is incapable of satisfactorily dealing with the economic imbalances that undermine the Eurozone (Collignon, 2009).

The results have been predictable, with passive fiscal policy and a tight monetary policy, preoccupied with price stabilisation, contributing to economic instability, unimpressive rates of economic growth and problems eradicating unemployment (Arestis and Sawyer, 1998: 181; Bibow, 2013: 619; Fitoussi and Saraceno, 2013: 484). Concerns raised at the time of EMU design, that the introduction of a single currency along these lines would result in a loss of flexibility, were largely dismissed. Yet time has vindicated this assessment (Krugman, 2012: 439). De Grauwe (2006: 711) summarises the position thus:

> The present governance of the euro area has been devised assuming that the world fits the monetarist-real-business-cycle theory. But that theory is not a correct representation of the world.

Krugman (2012: 443) largely echoes this opinion, when he writes:

> Even at the time, this sounded to many American economists like wishful thinking. After all, asymmetric shocks do not have to arise from unsound policies – they can come from shifts in relative product demand or, of course, such things as real estate bubbles. And European leaders seemed to believe that they could achieve a degree of wage flexibility that would be more or less unprecedented in the modern world.

The introduction of the single currency has additionally resulted in increased inequality, both within and between participating member states (Stiglitz, 2016: xviii, 13, 79). As a result, Stiglitz (2016: xviii) concludes that "the neo-liberal economic agenda may not have succeeded in increasing average growth rates, but of this we can be sure: it has succeeded in increasing inequality". Perhaps it is not a wonder, therefore, that one of the architects of neo-liberal economics considered it necessary to dismiss this evidence as irrelevant to the operation of a market economy, by stating that, "of the tendencies that are harmful to sound economics, the most seductive, and in my opinion the most poisonous is to focus on questions of distribution" (Lucas, 2003).

A faulty reaction to the Eurocrisis

The reaction to the recent Eurozone crisis illustrates why the neo-liberal approach fails to provide a sustainable basis for the development of EMU. Rather than considering whether the tensions within the Eurozone might arise from weaknesses within the design of EMU itself, conventional wisdom held that the fault lay in deficient policy or 'indiscipline' in deficit nations. In particular, budgetary policy was considered to have been too expansive and economies are too competitively inflexible (Blankenburg et al., 2013: 464–465). This conclusion was reinforced by assessments made by the financial markets, who caused the spreads to rise and this pressured those nations into austerity programmes to placate the markets (De Grauwe, 2013: 13–16).

These judgements were not necessarily even-handed, however, as the financial markets appeared to treat core (Northern) European economies more generously than periphery (Southern) European nations (De Grauwe, 2013: 17; Mazier and Valdecantos, 2015: 94). Moreover, since a significant proportion of public debt had been incurred as a result of the government bail-outs of the financial sector in the aftermath of the 2008 global financial crisis, it is rather perplexing that the finances of the state were subsequently criticised by the very financial sector that it had only just rescued (Whyman et al., 2012: 285). Nevertheless, rather than use the economic weight of the Eurozone to lean against such questionable market sentiment, the Commission and ECB exerted moral suasion in criticising debtor nations for their profligacy and insisting that they reduce budget deficits, though a combination of public expenditure cuts and increases in taxation, whilst declining international competitiveness would be solved through resultant declining real wages. Surplus nations were encouraged to pursue balanced budgets which made it even harder for deficit nations to reduce deficits and restore budget balance themselves (De Grauwe, 2013: 22).

Unfortunately, these conclusions ignored two pieces of evidence. The first is that it was misdiagnosed, even in its own terms as, prior to the financial crisis, both Ireland and Spain had budget surpluses, with only Greece displaying apparent financial mismanagement (Bird and Mandilaras, 2013). Hence, responses to the crisis have focused upon the symptom and not the fundamental causes (Calcagno, 2012: 24). In addition, the bitter medicine prescribed for the treatment of perceived profligacy ignored the fact that the ECB tolerates weak demand in the Eurozone which increases the difficulty in a nation deflating its way to restore competitiveness, particularly when those member states (particularly Germany) seek to maintain their own trade surpluses. It is a large rise in the external demand for their output that these economies require, rather than fiscal austerity.

The response to the Eurozone crisis highlighted weaknesses at the heart of EMU, and demonstrated how "exceptionally dysfunctional" its supportive policy framework had been in mitigating the worse effects of a period of adverse external shocks (Stockhammer, 2016: 367). Yet, rather than the European economic orthodoxy being challenged and rejected, as a result of the weak economic performance of the European economy during the monetary integration period, it has been reinforced through the introduction of the fiscal compact and troika imposing austerity upon those member states requiring loans from the European Stability Mechanism (Degryse, 2012: 67; Hein, 2013; Baimbridge and Whyman, 2015: 145–149; Stiglitz, 2016: 240–254).

This approach has, furthermore, been bolstered by adherents of 'expansionary austerity' theory, whereby fiscal consolidation is claimed to improve confidence and hence have favourable effects on growth in the medium to long term (Giavazzi and Pagano, 1990; Guarjardo et al., 2011; ECB, 2012: 85; Blyth, 2013; Perotti, 2011).[2] By contrast, empirical studies examining austerity programmes implemented in industrialised economies during the previous three decades, demonstrate that fiscal consolidation reduces growth and increases unemployment, particularly during periods when multiple nations, all in recession, reduce fiscal expenditures simultaneously (IMF, 2010: 94; Blanchard and Leigh, 2013).

A problem of trade imbalances not fiscal imbalances

Fiscal profligacy is not at the heart of the problems experienced in the Eurozone, but it is rather a symptom of a larger and more fundamental concern, namely the trade imbalances that are difficult to rectify within a neo-liberal variant of EMU (Bibow, 2013: 366–367). Trade imbalances have often proved to be fatal for previous forms of fixed exchange-rate systems, where this has not been adequately rectified. However, in the case of the Eurozone, which is after all a particular form of fixed exchange-rate system, this flaw is magnified by the dominance of one particular economy, Germany, whose growth strategy has complicated matters for all other Eurozone participants.

Germany has long pursued an export-led growth strategy, which combined the restraint of domestic demand whilst simultaneously promoting of internal discipline in order to maintain a lower rate of inflation than most other economies and hence enhance international competitiveness over time (Holtfrerich, 2008: 35). In the absence of countervailing changes in relative productivity, diverging wage and price growth erodes the competitive position of high- vis-á-vis low-inflation member states. Hence, by precluding adjustment through the nominal exchange rate, the Eurozone has been characterised by a growing trade imbalance, with Germany in particular running large trade surpluses, reaching 9 per cent of GDP in 2016, which was the largest in the world (Bibow, 2017: 32). In the process, Germany accumulated €1.2 trillion of net foreign assets since the turn of the century (Laski and Podkaminer, 2012: 257; Bibow, 2013: 623). Yet this version of is only possible because other member states amassed trade deficits through purchasing German exports. Thus, there is a symmetrical nature to the development of the Eurozone trade imbalance. Yet potential adjustment mechanisms are disproportionately imposed upon deficit nations.

The problem with this form of "supercharged mercantilism" (Bibow, 2013: 380), is that that the 'German model' works precisely when other nations do not behave the same as Germany. Export-led growth cannot be the solution for all economies simultaneously, due to simple mathematical certainty that if one nation runs a trade surplus, another must of necessity be running a deficit (Vernengo and Pérez-Caldentey, 2012). The German approach, therefore, only works when other nations do not seek to behave like Germany and deflate their economies in order to become more competitive and hence reduce their trade deficits (Bibow, 2017: 3, 24–25). Germany's desire to maintain its international competitiveness through economic restraint caused intraregional imbalances between Germany and other Eurozone participants. However, whilst there is a symmetrical cause to the Eurozone trade imbalances, the adjustment mechanisms adopted by neo-liberal EMU are disproportionately forced upon deficit economies, whether through fiscal austerity, designed to restrain wages and/ or the social wage in order to restore competitiveness, or alternatively through factor mobility (Weidmann, 2012).

This creates a deflationary bias at the heart of the Eurozone (Stockhammer, 2016: 367). These measures create social distress, as exhibited most potently in Greece, which undermines the social solidarity upon which the European project is based. Yet, the restoration of trade balance is further inhibited if surplus nations seek to maintain their export-led growth strategy and thereby impose the cost of adjustment asymmetrically upon deficit nations. Moreover, the asymmetric nature of adjustment reduces Eurozone aggregate demand as a whole (Stiglitz and Greenwald, 2010: 12). Whilst this may eventually reduce the exports of surplus nations, it does so only by reducing growth potential and increasing unemployment unnecessarily within the Eurozone. Even this wasteful method of securing adjustment only works if surplus nations do not seek to restore their surpluses, by seeking to enhance their own competitive position, and thereby worsening the position of deficit nations. This is a fundamental flaw at the heart of the current model of EMU (Blankenburg et al., 2013: 465–466; Hein, 2013: 326). The placement of all adjustment costs upon specific (that is, deficit) members has never worked in the long term as the periodic crises and the ultimate collapse of the silver and gold standards are evident proof (Eichengreen, 1996; Almunia et al., 2010).

Potential solutions?

The "utterly dysfunctional" nature of the monetarist variant of EMU necessitates fundamental reform if this aspect of the European project is to prove sustainable in the long term (Bibow, 2013: 618). This is a viewpoint shared by Collignon (2009: 188), who argues that the inability to fundamentally reform this approach will result in a profound malaise and "the European Union will die a slow death by gridlock, economic stagnation and unkept promises".

There have been a large number of suggestions for the reform of the current set of policy institutions established to sustain the single currency. These include proposals to introduce a system of fiscal federalism, to assist with long-term stabilisation (De Grauwe and Vanhaverbeke, 1993:112–125; Whyman, 2010; De Grauwe, 2013: 25–26) and the replacement of the current SGP with a 'Full Employment, Growth and Stability Pact', thereby neatly differentiating the proposed objectives of a Keynesian approach from the existing EMU neo-liberal model (Arestis, 1999: 9–10; Arestis et al., 2001). In addition, there have been propositions that improved governance and a shift towards political union are necessary measures to ensure the single currency has sufficient political legitimacy and can facilitate supranational control over fiscal policy (Kaldor, 1978: 206; Artis, 2009; De Grauwe, 2006: 711, 2009).

Another option involves the reconfiguring the single currency in terms of its membership, through allowing or encouraging struggling member states to withdraw. There are a number of historical precedents concerning how currency unions can be dissolved and how individual nations can withdraw from such arrangements. These examples range from the disintegration of the Austro-Hungarian Empire after the First World War to, more recently, the separation of the former Soviet Union and 'velvet divorce' between the Czech and Slovak republics. The ease of currency separation was variable in each of these cases; for the former Soviet Union the transition was economically difficult, whereas for the Czech and Slovak korunas, the process was considerably more straightforward. Partly this reflected technical solutions to managing the process and partly concerning the ability of the political processes to manage the dissolution of former supranational entities. Nevertheless, exchange control restrictions proved necessary to prevent financial dislocations and facilitate these processes, whilst the process was further aided by the less developed nature of the banking systems in each of these nation states (Eichengreen, 2010: 23–26).

This process might be more difficult for the Eurozone, because of what former Greek Finance Minister Varoufakis (2016: 142) describes as the current EMU model creating a "Hotel California" situation which, like the song by the band The Eagles, makes it difficult if not impossible to ever leave. Given that the creation of an alternative currency would take time to print and distribute, and that banks and businesses would need an adjustment period to recalibrate their accounting and payment systems to work with the new currency, there would exist an incentive for capital flight in advance of the eventual devaluation, thereby destabilising the economy and exacerbating any short-term instability. In addition, indebted states have been encouraged to borrow in Euros and hence, were the reestablishment of a national currency to coincide with a devaluation, this would increase the amount of this now foreign-denominated debt. As a result, Varoufakis argues that the current Eurozone arrangements constrain potential exit for those participants whose economies suffer the most from continued membership.

This conclusion is a little exaggerated in the sense that technological advances and shifts to electronic payment systems have made it possible to change prices and other accounts more easily and with shorter time lags to introduce new currencies than in former time periods, when economic actors were more heavily reliant upon physical coinage and businesses more reliant upon printed brochures. Moreover, since EMU does allow a temporary imposition of exchange controls, where severe economic destabilisation could result which may undermine the single currency as a whole, this would provide temporary breathing space for national policy changes.

Whilst the unilateral withdrawal of certain outlier member states from EMU membership, who never met the convergence criteria on a sustainable basis in any case, would solve the worst problems of the Eurozone in the short run, the fundamental design flaws would remain and impose future costs upon another member state finding itself an outlier at some future point. Thus, the inability or unwillingness of surplus nations to share part of the necessary adjustment that is a common feature of currency arrangements between sovereign nations is the flaw which tends to undermine their long-term sustainability.

It would, however, certainly be a superior option for the Eurozone, as a whole, to consider fundamental reforms which allowed for the type of changes to be suggested in the following chapters. Altering the system as a whole would leave individual member states less exposed to capital flight and the reaction of international financial markets. It would also maintain the solidarity between nations that is supposed to lie at the heart of the European project.

Conclusion

The introduction of the single European currency was intended to encourage higher economic growth and foster closer co-operation between the people of Europe. The truly (Greek) tragedy of the recent history is that it has done the opposite, whilst inflicting devastating economic consequences upon many European citizens. The crisis has demonstrated the defective design of EMU, but it has also revealed, and exacerbated, a fundamental lack of trust, let alone a source of shared identity, among the peoples locked together, in what has become a marriage of inconvenience (Baimbridge and Whyman, 2015: 20). Even the cautious advocate of the potential benefits of EMU, De Grauwe (2006: 728), felt compelled to issue the following warning over the inability of the reform measures to tackle the fundamental problems affecting the Eurozone, by stating:

> It is difficult to conceive how a union can be politically sustainable if each and every time a country of the union gets into trouble because of asymmetric developments, it is told by the other members that it is entirely its own fault and that it should not count on any help. Such a union will not last.

In the absence of fundamental structural reform, preferably along the lines advocated by Keynes seventy years before, it is difficult to conceive how the current model of EMU can be sustainable in the long term. It is to that fundamental reform, and the creation of a progressive model of EMU that might actually achieve its fundamental objectives, that the next chapter focuses.

Notes

1 Speech given by Sirka Hamalainen, executive member of the European Central Bank Board, at the Finnish Chamber of Commerce. The talk was entitled 'What Are the Benefits of the Single Currency for Competition and Growth in the Euro Area'. Available via: www.ecb.europa.eu/press/key/date/2000/html/sp001007.en.html (accessed 22 November 2017).
2 This hypothesis is examined in greater detail in Chapter 4 of this book.

Bibliography

Alexiou, C. and Pitelis, C. (2003), 'On Capital Shortages and European Unemployment: A Panel Data Investigation', *Journal of Post Keynesian Economics*, 25(4): 613–631.
Almunia, M., Bénétrix, A., Eichengreen, B., O'Rourke, K.H. and Rua, G. (2010), 'From Great Depression to Great Credit Crisis: Similarities, Differences and Lessons', *Economic Policy*, 25(62): 219–265.
Alves, A.J., Ferrari Jr, F. and De Paula, L.F.R. (1999), 'The Post Keynesian Critique of Conventional Currency Crisis Models and Davidson's Proposal to Reform the International Monetary System', *Journal of Post Keynesian Economics*, 22(2): 207–225.

Arestis, P. (1999), 'The Independent European Central Bank: Keynesian Alternatives', *Jerome Levy Economics Institute Working Paper* No. 274.

Arestis, P. and Mariscal, I. (1997), 'Conflict, Effort and Capital Stock in UK Wage Determination', *Empirica*, 24(3): 179–193.

Arestis, P., McCauley, K. and Sawyer, M. (2001), 'An Alternative Stability Pact for the European Union', *Cambridge Journal of Economics*, 25(1): 113–130.

Arestis, P. and Sawyer, M. (1998), 'Keynesian Policies for the New Millennium', *Economic Journal*, 108(446): 181–195.

Arestis, P. and Sawyer, M. (2004), *Re-Examining Monetary and Fiscal Policy for the 21st Century*, Edward Elgar, Cheltenham.

Artis, M. (2009), 'Globalisation vs. Europeanisation: Assessing the Impact of EMU on Business Cycle Affiliation', in Talini, L. (Ed.), *The Future of EMU*, Palgrave, Basingstoke, 75–88.

Backhouse, R. (2009), 'Economists and the Rise of Neo-Liberalism', *Renewal: A Journal of Social Democracy*, 17(4): 17–25. Available via: www.renewal.org.uk/articles/economists-and-the-rise-of-neo-liberalism.

Baddeley, M.C. (2003), *Investment: Theories and Analysis*, Palgrave, Basingstoke.

Baimbridge, M., Burkitt, B. and Whyman, P.B. (1998), 'Is Europe Ready for EMU?', *Occasional Paper* No. 31, Bruges Group, London.

Baimbridge, M., Burkitt, B. and Whyman, P.B. (1999), 'Economic Convergence and EMU Membership: Theory and Evidence', *Journal of European Integration*, 21(4): 281–305.

Baimbridge, M., Burkitt, B. and Whyman, P.B. (2012), 'The Eurozone as a Flawed Currency Area', *Political Quarterly*, 83(1): 96–107.

Baimbridge, M. and Whyman, P.B. (2008), *Britain, the Euro and Beyond*, Ashgate, Aldershot.

Baimbridge, M. and Whyman, P.B. (2015), *Crisis in the Eurozone: Causes, Dilemmas and Solutions*, Palgrave, Basingstoke.

Baker, D. (2000), 'Something New in the 1990s: Looking for Evidence of an Economic Transformation', in Marick, J. (Ed.), *Unconventional Wisdom: Alternative Perspectives on the New Economy*, Century Foundation Press, New York, 207–237.

Ball, L. (1994), 'Disinflation and the NAIRU', in Romer, C. and Romer, D. (Eds.), *Reducing Inflation: Motivation and Strategy*, University of Chicago Press, Chicago.

Barba, A. and De Vivo, G. (2013), 'Flawed Currency Areas and Viable Currency Areas: External Imbalances and Public Finance in the Time of the Euro', *Contributions to Political Economy*, 32(1): 73–96.

Barro, R. and Gordon, D. (1983), 'Rules, Discretion, and Reputation in a Model of Monetary Policy', *Journal of Monetary Economics*, 12(1): 101–121.

Bayoumi, T. and Eichengreen, B. (1993), 'Shocking Aspects of European Monetary Integration', in Torres, F. and Giavazzi, F. (Eds.), *Adjustment and Growth in the European Monetary Union*, Cambridge University Press, Cambridge, 193–229.

Bean, C. (1989), 'Capital Shortages and Persistent Unemployment', *Economic Policy*, 8: 11–53.

Bean, C. (1994), 'European Unemployment: A Retrospective', *European Economic Review*, 38(3–4): 523–534.

Bibow, J. (2013), 'The Euroland Crisis and Germany's Euro Trilemma', *International Review of Applied Economics*, 27(3): 360–385.

Bibow, J. (2017), 'How Germany's Anti-Keynesianism Has Brought Europe to Its Knees', *Levy Economics Institute Working Paper* No. 886. Available via: www.levyinstitute.org/publications/how-germanys-anti-keynesianism-has-brought-europe-to-its-knees.

Bird, G. and Mandilaras, A. (2012), 'Will Europe's Fiscal Compact Help Avoid Future Economic Crises?', *University of Surrey Discussion Papers in Economics*, DP 12/12. Available via: www.surrey.ac.uk/sites/default/files/DP12-12.pdf.

Bird, G. and Mandilaras, A. (2013), 'Fiscal Imbalances and Output Crises in Europe: Will the Fiscal Compact Help or Hinder?', *Journal of Economic Policy Reform*, 16(1): 1–16.

Blanchard, O.J. and Leigh, D. (2013), 'Growth Forecast Errors and Fiscal Multipliers', *International Monetary Fund Working Paper* No. WP/13/1.

Blanchard, O.J. and Summers, L. (1988), 'Beyond the Natural Rate Hypothesis', *American Economic Review*, 78(2): 182–187.

Blankenburg, S., King, L., Konzelmann, S. and Wilkinson, F. (2013), 'Prospects for the Eurozone', *Cambridge Journal of Economics*, 37(3): 463–477.

Blyth, M. (2013), *Austerity: The History of a Dangerous Idea*, Oxford University Press, Oxford.

Boyer, R. (2013), 'The Euro Crisis: Undetected by Conventional Economics, Favoured by Nationally Focused Polity', *Cambridge Journal of Economics*, 37(3): 533–569.

Calcagno, A. (2012), 'Can Austerity Work?', *Review of Keynesian Economics*, 1(1): 24–36.

Collignon, S. (2009), 'The Lisbon Strategy, Macroeconomic Stability and the Dilemma of Governance With Governments (Or Why Europe Is Not Becoming the World's Most Dynamic Economy)', in Talini, L.S. (Ed.), *The Future of EMU*, Palgrave, Basingstoke, 161–193.

Cowling, K. (1987), 'An Industrial Strategy for Britain', *International Review of Applied Economics*, 1: 1–22.

Davidson, P. (1998), 'Post Keynesian Employment Analysis and the Macroeconomics of OECD Unemployment', *The Economic Journal*, 108(2): 817–831.

De Grauwe, P. (2006), 'What Have We Learnt About Monetary Union Since the Maastricht Treaty?', *Journal of Common Market Studies*, 44(4): 711–730.

De Grauwe, P. (2009), 'Some Thoughts on Monetary and Political Union', in Talini, L. (Ed.), *The Future of EMU*, Palgrave, Basingstoke, 9–29.

De Grauwe, P. (2013), 'Design Failures in the Eurozone: Can They Be Fixed?', *European Economy Economics Papers*, No. 491, European Commission, Brussels. Available via: http://ec.europa.eu/economy_finance/publications/economic_paper/2013/pdf/ecp491_en.pdf.

De Grauwe, P. and Vanhaverbeke, W. (1993), 'Is Europe an Optimum Currency Area?', in Masson, P.R. and Taylor, M.P. (Eds.), *Policy Issues in the Operation of Currency Unions*, Cambridge University Press, Cambridge, 111–129.

Degryse, C. (2012), 'The New Economic Governance', *ETUI Working Paper* No. 14.

Dyson, K. and Featherstone, K. (1999), *The Road to Maastricht: Negotiating EMU*, Oxford University Press, Oxford.

ECB [European Central Bank] (2012), 'The Role of Fiscal Multipliers in the Current Consolidation Debate', *ECB Monthly Bulletin*, 14(12): 82–85.

Eichengreen, B. (1990), 'One Money for Europe? Lessons From the US Currency Union', *Economic Policy*, 10: 117–188.

Eichengreen, B. (1992), 'Is Europe an Optimum Currency Area?', in Borner, S. and Grubel, H. (Eds.), *The European Community After 1992: Perspectives From the Outside*, Macmillan, London, 138–161.

Eichengreen, B. (1993), 'European Monetary Unification', *Journal of Economic Literature*, 31: 1321–1357.

Eichengreen, B. (1996), *Golden Fetters: The Gold Standard and the Great Depression, 1919–1939*, Oxford University Press, Oxford.

Eichengreen, B. (2010), 'The Breakup of the Euro Area', in Alesina, A. and Giavazzi, F. (Eds.), *Europe and the Euro*, University of Chicago Press and NBER, Chicago, 11–51.

EU [European Union] (2012), *Consolidated Versions of the Treaty on European Union and the Treaty on the Functioning of the European Union*, Official Journal C326/01, Article 127(1), European Commission, Brussels. Available via: http://eur-lex.europa.eu/legal-content/EN/TXT/?uri=CELEX:12012E/TXT.

Feldstein, M. (1997), 'The Political Economy of the European Economic and Monetary Union: Political Sources of an Economic Liability', *Journal of Economic Perspectives*, 11(4): 23–42.

Fitoussi, J.-P. and Saraceno, F. (2013), 'European Economic Governance: The Berlin – Washington Consensus', *Cambridge Journal of Economics*, 37(3): 479–496.

Frankel, J.A. (1999), 'No Single Currency Regime is Right for All Countries or at All Times', *NBER Working Paper* No. 7338. Available via: www.nber.org/papers/w7338.

Friedman, M. (1968), 'The Role of Monetary Policy', *American Economic Review*, 58: 1–17.

Galbraith, J.K. (1997), 'Time to Ditch the NAIRU', *Journal of Economic Perspectives*, 11(1): 93–108.

Giavazzi, F. and Pagano, M. (1990), 'Can Severe Fiscal Contractions Be Expansionary? Tales of Two Small European Countries', in Blanchard, O.J. and Fischer, S. (Eds.), *NBER Macroeconomics Annual 1990*, Volume 5, MIT Press, Boston, MA, 75–122.

Gordon, R. (1997), 'The Time-Varying NAIRU and Its Implications for Economic Policy', *Journal of Economic Perspectives*, 11(1): 11–32.

Guajardo, J., Leigh, D. and Pescatori, A. (2011), 'Expansionary Austerity: New International Evidence', *IMF Working Paper* No. WP/11/158. Available via: www.imf.org/external/pubs/ft/wp/2011/wp11158.pdf.

Hein, E. (2013), 'Finance-Dominated Capitalism and Redistribution of Income: A Kaleckian Perspective', *Levy Economics Institute of Bard College Working Paper* No. 746.

Hein, E. (2017), 'An Alternative Macroeconomic Policy for the Eurozone', in Herr, H., Priewe, J. and Watt, A. (Eds.), *Saving the Euro: Redesigning Euro Area Economic Governance*, S.E. Publishing, London, 61–81.

Hemerijck, A. and Ferrera, M. (2004), 'Welfare Reform in the Shadow of EMU', in Martin, A. and Ross, G. (Eds.), *Euros and Europeans: Monetary Integration and the European Model of Society*, Cambridge University Press, Cambridge, 248–277.

HOL [House of Lords] (2007), 'The Impact of Economic and Monetary Union to Date', in Select Committee on European Union, *European Union: Thirteenth Report*, Chapter Three. Available via: https://publications.parliament.uk/pa/ld200708/ldselect/ldeucom/90/9006.htm.

Holtfrerich, C.L. (2008), 'Monetary Policy in Germany Since 1948: National Tradition, International Best Practice or Ideology?', in Touffut, J.P. (Ed.), *Central Banks as Economic Institutions*, Edward Elgar, Cheltenham, 22–51.

IMF [International Monetary Fund] (2010), 'Will It Hurt? Macroeconomic Effects of Fiscal Consolidation', in *World Economic Outlook: Recovery, Risk, and Rebalancing*, International Monetary Fund, Washington, DC, 93–124.

Kaldor, N. (1970), 'The Case for Regional Policies', *Scottish Journal of Political Economy*, 17(3): 337–348.

Kaldor, N. (1972), 'The Irrelevance of Equilibrium Economics', *Economic Journal*, 82(328): 1237–1255.

Kaldor, N. (1978), 'The Dynamic Effects of the Common Market', in Kaldor, N. (Ed.), *Further Essays of Applied Economics*, Duckworth, London, 187–220.

Kaldor, N. (1981), 'The Role of Increasing Returns, Technical Progress and Cumulative Causation in the Theory of International Trade and Economic Growth', *Économie Appliquée*, 34(4): 593–617.

Keynes, J.M. (1936), *The General Theory of Employment, Interest and Money*, Macmillan, Basingstoke, 1973 edition.

Krugman, P. (1993), 'Lessons of Massachusetts for EMU', in Giavazzi, F. and Torres, F. (Eds.), *The Transition to Economic and Monetary Union in Europe*, Cambridge University Press, Cambridge, 241–261.

Krugman, P. (1999), *The Return of Depression Economics*, Penguin, London, revised 2000 edition.

Krugman, P. (2012), 'Revenge of the Optimum Currency Area', *NBER Macroeconomics Annual*, 27(1): 439–448. Available via: www.nber.org/chapters/c12759.pdf.

Kyland, F. and Prescott, E. (1977), 'Rules Rather Than Discretion: The Inconsistency of Optimal Plans', *Journal of Political Economy*, 85(3): 473–492.

Lane, P.R. (2012), 'The European Sovereign Debt Crisis', *Journal of Economic Perspectives*, 26(3): 49–68.

Laski, K. and Podkaminer, L. (2012), 'The Basic Paradigms of EU Economic Policy-Making Need to Be Changed', *Cambridge Journal of Economics*, 36(1): 253–270.

Lavoie, M. (2015), 'The Eurozone: Similarities to and Differences From Keynes's Plan', *International Journal of Political Economy*, 44(1): 3–17.

Layard, R. and Nickell, S. (1985), 'The Causes of British Unemployment', *National Economic Institute Review*, 111: 62–85.

Lucas, R.E. (1976), 'Econometric Policy Evaluation: A Critique', in Brunner, K. and Meltzer, A. (Eds.), *Carnegie-Rochester Series in Public Policy*, North-Holland, Amsterdam.

Lucas, R.E. (2003), *The Industrial Revolution: Past and future*, Federal Reserve Bank of Minneapolis. Available via: www.minneapolisfed.org/publications/the-region/the-industrial-revolution-past-and-future.

Mazier, J. and Valdecantos, S. (2015), 'A Multi-Speed Europe: Is It Viable? A Stock Flow Consistent Approach', *European Journal of Economics and Economic Policies: Intervention*, 12(1): 93–112.

Moss, B. (2005), 'The EU as a Neo-Liberal Construction', in Moss, B. (Ed.), *Monetary Union in Crisis: The European Union as a Neo-Liberal Construction*, Palgrave, Basingstoke, 1–26.

Mundell, R.A. (1961), 'A Theory of Optimum Currency Areas', *American Economic Review*, 51(4): 657–665.

Myrdal, G. (1957), *Economic Theory and Underdeveloped Regions*, Duckworth, London.

Perotti, R. (2011), 'The "Austerity Myth": Gain Without Pain', *NBER Working Paper* No. 17571. Available via: www.nber.org/papers/w17571.

Phelps, E.S. (1968), 'Money-Wage Dynamics and Labor Market Equilibrium', *Journal of Political Economy*, 76(4S): 678–711.

Rowthorn, R.E. (1995), 'Capital Formation and Unemployment', *Oxford Review of Economic Policy*, 11(1): 26–39.

Rowthorn, R.E. (1999), 'Unemployment, Wage Bargaining and Capital-Labour Substitution', *Cambridge Journal of Economics*, 23(3): 413–425.

Sapir, A., Aghion, P., Bertola, G., Hellwig, M., Pisani-Ferry, J., Rosati, D., Vinals, J. and Wallace, H. (2004), *An Agenda for a Growing Europe: The Sapir Report*, Oxford University Press, Oxford.

Sawyer, M. (2003), 'The NAIRU, Labour Market "Flexibility" and Full Employment', in Stanford, J. and Vosko, L. (Eds.), *Challenging the Market: The Struggle to Regulate Work and Income*, McGill-Queen's University Press, Belfast.

Setterfield, M., Gordon, D.V. and Osberg, L. (1992), 'Searching for a Will o' Wisp: An Empirical Study of the NAIRU in Canada', *European Economic Review*, 36(1): 119–136.

Skidelsky, R. (2005), 'Keynes, Globalisation and the Bretton Woods Institutions in the Light of Changing Ideas About Markets', *World Economics*, 6(1): 5–30.

Smithin, J. and Wolf, B.M. (1993), 'What Would Be a "Keynesian" Approach to Currency and Exchange Rate Issues?', *Review of Political Economy*, 5(3): 365–383.

Stiglitz, J. (2003), *The Roaring Nineties: Seeds of Destruction*, Penguin, London.

Stiglitz, J.A. (2016), *The Euro and Its Threat to the Future of Europe*, Allen Lane, London.

Stiglitz, J.E. and Greenwald, B. (2010), 'Towards a New Global Reserve System', *Journal of Globalisation and Development*, 1(2): 1–24.

Stockhammer, E. (2016), 'Neo-Liberal Growth Models, Monetary Union and the Euro Crisis: A Post-Keynesian Perspective', *New Political Economy*, 21(4): 365–379.

UNCTAD [United Nations Conference on Trade and Development] (1995), *World Investment Report 1995*, United Nations.

Varoufakis, Y. (2016), *And the Weak Suffer What They Must? Europe, Austerity and the Threat to Global Stability*, The Global Minotaur, Penguin-Random House, London.

Verdun, A. (1996), 'An Asymmetrical Economic and Monetary Union in the EU: Perceptions of Monetary Authorities and Social Partners', *Revue d'intégration européene/Journal of European Integration*, 20(1): 59–81.

Vernengo, M. and Pérez-Caldentey, E. (2012), 'The Euro Imbalances and Financial Deregulation: A Post Keynesian Interpretation of the European Debt Crisis', *Real-World Economics Review*, 59: 83–104.

Weber, A.A. (1991), 'EMU and Asymmetries and Adjustment Problems in the EMS', in 'The Economics of EMU', *European Economy*, Special Edition 1, 44(1): 187–207.

Weidmann, J. (2012), *Rebalancing Europe*. Speech, London, March 28, BIS Central Bankers' Speeches. Available via: www.bis.org/review/r120329a.pdf.

Whyman, P.B. (2010), 'Stabilising Economic and Monetary Union in Europe: The Potential for a Semi-Automatic Stabilisation Mechanism', in Tavidze, A. (Ed.), *Progress in Economics Research, Volume 18*, Nova Science Publishers, Hauppauge, NY, 1–26.

Whyman, P.B., Baimbridge, M. and Mullen, A. (2012), *The Political Economy of the European Social Model*, Routledge, Abingdon.

Zarotiadis, G. and Gkagka, A. (2013), 'European Union: A Diverging Union?', *Journal of Post Keynesian Economics*, 35(4): 537–565.

2 Single currency or common currency?

> I believe that the only important structural obstacles to world prosperity are the obsolete doctrines that clutter the minds of men.
>
> (Krugman, 1999: 168)

Introduction

The previous chapter highlighted a number of the weaknesses inherent within the particular model of EMU chosen as the basis for the single currency within the European Union. These flaws were always likely to create problems sustaining the Eurozone in the medium to long term, due to the persistence of asymmetric shocks and a secondary asymmetry in placing the burden of adjustment to economic instability disproportionately upon those nations already struggling with the consequences of trade imbalances. However, the chosen response of the EU to the 2008 global financial crisis, and the subsequent Eurozone crisis, have further retrenched many of these problems and exacerbated potential future instability. The financial crisis has not *caused* these problems but rather has *magnified* or highlighted the existence of pre-existing weaknesses which have long been recognised by a selection of the academic commentators who have written on this topic over the past two decades (Eichengreen, 1992; De Grauwe and Vanhaverbeke, 1993; Burkitt et al., 1996; Arestis and Sawyer, 2000; Degryse, 2012: 6).

The EU's response to the Eurocrisis, combining emergency loans and the new 'fiscal compact' (EU Commission, 2011; Degryse, 2012)[1] is, at best, likely to be a temporary relief for Eurozone members, as it does not address some of the fundamental issues inherent within any fixed (or single) currency arrangement. It does not, for example, provide sufficient stabilisation for the single currency zone, given the persistence of asymmetric shocks (Bayoumi and Eichengreen, 1993; De Grauwe and Vanhaverbeke, 1993: 112–125). Similarly, the policy reforms fail to deal with large, persistent payments imbalances between participating member states (Stiglitz and Greenwald, 2010: 12). Given that the adoption of a single currency precludes the use of the exchange rate as an ameliorating instrument, it is therefore self-evident that shifts in international competitiveness are more difficult to resolve, except through deficit nations adopting general deflationary measures and/or policies aimed at reducing real or social wages (Keynes, 1980a: 29).

There is, however, an alternative approach that could be adapted to the Euro-zone, and which would promote an agenda favouring employment and growth, rather than fiscal retrenchment and deflation. It would promote social cohesion and solidarity between member states, by imposing symmetrical responsibilities upon surplus as well as deficit nations. It would resolve many of the fundamental structural weaknesses with the current form of EMU, and thereby enhance the medium-term sustainability of the Eurozone.

This approach is not, in its fundamentals, particularly new. It draws heavily upon a set of proposals made by John Maynard Keynes in a UK government white paper published in 1942, as his contribution to the discussions which eventually led to the development of the Bretton Woods post-war economic settlement (Keynes, 1980b; Skidelsky, 2000, 2005: 15–16; Steil, 2013). Moreover, these ideas reflected earlier work completed by Keynes (1923, 1930, 1933) in the aftermath of the collapse of the Gold Standard after the First World War, where his concern focused upon the problems of open economies seeking to balance simultaneously both internal and external equilibrium. His attention was upon providing a means of managing the international payments system to prevent persistent deflationary episodes caused by trade imbalances (Smithin and Wolf, 1993: 368–370). The result was the development of the 1942 Keynes Plan, where a supranational central bank presided over an international payments system designed to share the burden of adjustment between debtor and creditor nations, rather than simply the former.

The elegant solution produced by Keynes to solve the problems of an earlier age would appear to be almost tailor made to resolve many of the weaknesses inherent in the current model of EMU (Varoufakis, 2015: 60). Indeed, even the former head of the IMF, Dominique Strass-Kahn, has advocated its adoption as a potential solution to the problems of the global economy in the aftermath of the 2008 financial crisis.[2]

Keynes was concerned that economic integration without a sufficiently supportive macroeconomic policy framework could result in damage to national economies and potentially the collapse of the integration project itself (Skidelsky, 2005: 19). This is precisely the position in which the Eurozone currently finds itself. His solution would promote closer economic integration between participating nations without systematic trade imbalances forcing ultimately unsustainable deflation upon member states running trade deficits, and thereby causing the whole of the Eurozone area to operate at less than its full employment optimum. This chapter, therefore, draws upon Keynes's proposals for an International Currency Union (ICU), and adapts them to the particular circumstances faced by the Eurozone. This would involve the replacement of a *single* currency with a *common* currency approach, combined with significant reform to the economic institutions intended to support this alternative variant of EMU.

The Keynes International Clearing Union (ICU) Plan

As befits his broader focus upon inadequate effective demand and the under-employment of resources, Keynes proposed a form of international monetary system which combined the benefits of fixed exchange rates with an attempt to secure an expansionist (rather than contractionist) pressure on world trade and international balances (Keynes, 1980a: 77, 143). Reduction in exchange rate uncertainty was expected to facilitate increased investment, trade and ultimately economic growth. In the same way that a withdrawal from the circular flow of income reduces aggregate demand in a particular country and thereby poten-tially results in under-employment equilibria, Keynes registered concern over the inability for an international payments system to prevent excess reserves from withdrawing money from the global economy (Keynes, 1980a: 74–75). If unwarranted by reasonable risk assessment, the build-up of excessive reserves equates to hoarding (Keynes, 1980a: 273). If surpluses were to remain unused, as would be the case in mercantilist strategy, the result would be a sub-optimal level of aggregate demand, insufficient to maintain full employment.

Attempts made by deficit nations to restore balance would exacerbate this problem, through deflation and other adjustment programmes (Piffaretti, 2009b: 47). Domestic deflation and devaluation, both of which seek to reduce the international price of exports relative to imports, with the elasticities of demand for imported and exported goods and services determining whether a modest or very large correction would be required to restore balance (Keynes, 1980a: 29). Deflation would reduce the demand for imports, as a result of declining wages (or the social wage, via reductions in welfare expenditure) and/or increasing unemployment, whilst devaluation would make exports cheaper overseas and encourage import-substitution at home.

The ICU proposal, therefore, sought to devise an international monetary structure which would dissuade (or prevent) nations from pursuing mercantil-ism and thereby facilitate national aggregate demand management to secure full employment (Bibow, 2010: 26). If all nations maintained levels of expendi-ture sufficient to secure full employment, this should, in turn, lower the prob-ability of individual nations suffering persistent balance of payments weakness (Kalecki, 1946: 323–327). Net foreign expenditure would be financed through international long-term lending which would itself be facilitated through the introduction of an international investment office. Hence, "the plan aims at the substitution of an expansionist, in place of a contractionist, pressure on world trade" (Keynes, 1942; Keynes, 1980a: 46–48, 74–77).

The ICU proposal sought to establish an international system of payments which facilitated global full employment. The proposal had six main elements, namely:

1 Establishment of a currency union, based on international bank money
2 Creation of a closed payments system, enabling central banks to regulate the flow of international payments

3   Restrictions upon speculative and other short-term flows of capital
4   The need for symmetric not asymmetric rebalancing
5   Ensuring that international reserves are limited and re-circulated
6   Ability to readjust fixed exchange-rate values to reflect changes in effi-
    ciency wages.

These features individual features are combined to form the ICU model, which
can be viewed in Figure 2.1.

'Bancor' currency union

The ICU would utilise a form of international bank money, which Keynes
termed 'bancor' but which, in the context of the EU, could easily be renamed
as Euro-bancor. This would be fixed, at least nominally in terms of gold, with
national currencies fixed in relation to the bancor and thereby simultaneously
pegged in relation to one another. The purpose of the new currency would be
to settle international balances between participating member states, through
accounts maintained by national central banks. Those nations with a surplus
on their balance of payments account, with respect to other ICU participants,
would accrue a credit account, whereas those with a balance of payments deficit would generate a debit account (Davidson, 2009). Bancor would not necessarily be utilised for all transactions between individual businesses or banks, but
rather would be the sole means of settling the *final outstanding balances* between
the central banks of each participating nation.

   The supply of bancor was to be perfectly elastic up to the maximum set
for each country (Meltzer, 1983: 17), whilst the provision of foreign exchange
would be located solely within the central bank of each participating nation
(Keynes, 1980a: 33–34, 125). There would be one-way convertibility only, from
gold or national currencies to bancor (Keynes, 1942, 1980a: 95, 140). Thus, bancor reserves never leave the system, thereby negating the possibility of a run on
the currency (Arestis, 1999: 7). Furthermore, one of the main design features of
the bancor system was the attempt to avoid the accumulation of inactive balances held in individual national reserves and thereby preventing excess reserves
from unnecessarily withdrawing money from the Eurozone economy (Keynes,
1980a: 74–75, 273; Stiglitz and Greenwald, 2010). Bancor was, therefore, meant
to be a means of payment but not a store of value (Meltzer, 1983: 17; Alves
et al., 1999: 222–223).

Creation of a closed payments system

The purpose of the ICU would be to extend the banking principle that exists
within any closed system, namely that the sum of credits and debits (assets
and liabilities) must balance (Keynes, 1980a: 44, 72, 201). If credits (with-
drawals) are not permitted to exit the system, then the ICU will form the
equivalent of its own circular flow of income (Alves et al., 1999: 222–223).

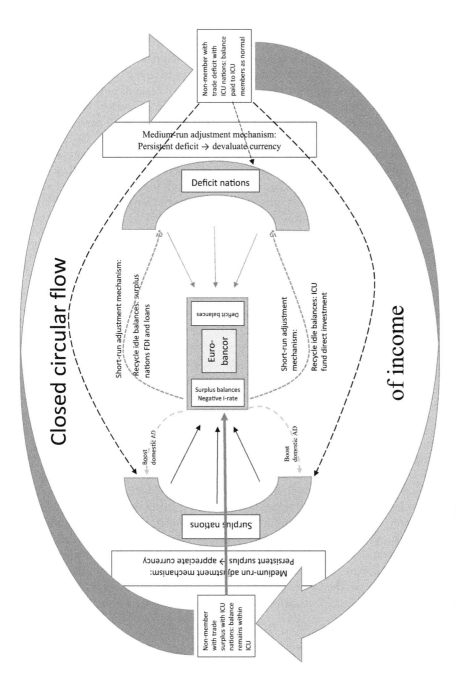

Figure 2.1 The Euro-ICU model

Consequently, aggregate demand across the Eurozone could be sustained at a sufficient level to maintain full employment (Keynes, 1980a: 44, 72; Davidson, 1982: 223; Arestis, 1999: 7).

To ensure that the payments system remained closed, the provision of foreign exchange would be located solely within the central bank of each participating nation. Where requested by individuals or businesses, other domestic banks would be required to apply to the central banks for release of these funds. This could operate through intermediaries, through a system of licences, but the settlement of ultimate outstanding balances would occur between central banks, which would have unqualified control over outward transactions of national citizens (Keynes, 1980a: 33–34, 125). The focal position of central banks within the ICU proposal largely reflected the position pertaining in the UK at the time Keynes was drafting the ICU proposals, although it would require a significant reversal of contemporary practice, where international financial markets operate without this restraint.

Capital controls

A closed payments system would require the re-introduction of capital controls, to prevent unregulated flows from undermining the ICU system. Indeed, Keynes (1980a: 30–31, 52, 65, 86–87, 129–130, 148–150, 185–186) argued that "nothing is more certain" than the need for "central control of capital movements, both inward and outward" to be a "permanent feature of the post war system", requiring "exchange control for *all* transactions". Payments arising from trade would be automatically permitted, and capital flows financing fixed investment would be treated more favourably than speculative capital flows, which would be prohibited (Keynes, 1980a: 52–53, 87, 212–213; Riese, 2008: 39). Hence, an ICU would eliminate what may be regarded as the "wasteful" foreign exchange activities of multinational banks, thereby curbing speculation and reducing the volatility in currencies that hamper economic activity in the real economy (D'Arista, 2003: 737; Lavoie, 2015: 5–7).

Meltzer (1983: 23) argued that Keynes had become convinced that no international monetary system was capable of achieving internal and external stability, high employment and economic freedom, and therefore he chose to sacrifice freedom through the introduction of a permanent system of exchange controls. The combination of fixed but adjustable exchange rates, capital controls and multilateral clearing, was intended to smooth the trade cycle and facilitate the expansion of trade, thereby setting the foundations for the maintenance of an expansionist and not a contractionist global economy. With idle balances being put to productive use, an ICU, protected by capital controls, could facilitate a higher level of international effective demand without inflationary consequences (Keynes, 1980a: 155). Higher international aggregate demand should further ease the pressure on deficit nations, thereby reducing tensions in the international payments system. Capital controls would, moreover, facilitate domestic macroeconomic management (Meltzer, 1983: 14–15).

Symmetric rebalancing

Given that the sum of the worldwide balance of payments must be zero, such that the sum of all surpluses must equal the sum of all deficits within a set period of time, surpluses cannot exist without an equivalent deficit occurring elsewhere in the world. Therefore, if the latter are a problem, the former must be a significant contributor to this problem occurring and persisting. This should imply that both surplus and deficit countries should be treated equally, in seeking to eliminate such trade imbalances, but this is not typically the case. Since problems with debtor countries can only occur, according to Keynes, if creditor countries are not making full use of the purchasing power derived from their trade surplus, therefore surplus countries are guilty of exporting deflationary consequences to other nations (Richardson, 1985: 24; Stiglitz and Greenwald, 2010: 6–7).

The original ICU proposals included a system of incentives and penalties, to be imposed on both deficit and surplus countries, and meant to discourage disequilibria (Costabile, 2010: 18–19; Keynes, 1980a: 78–81; Davidson, 1994: 268–272; Laski and Podkaminer, 2012: 269; Schiaffino, 2013). Deficit countries typically endure compulsion to reduce trade imbalances, whilst surplus countries generally evade similar pressure to change their behaviour. Yet, since problems with debtor countries can only occur, according to Keynes, if creditor countries are not making full use of the purchasing power derived from their trade surplus, then it must follow that surplus countries are guilty of exporting deflationary consequences to other nations (Keynes, 1980a; Richardson, 1985: 24; Stiglitz and Greenwald, 2010: 6–7).

In this endeavour, the ICU would mimic the actions of national central banks in pursuing international 'symmetric rebalancing', and thereby achieving simultaneous debtor and creditor adjustment without forcing ultimately unsustainable deflation upon weaker member states (Piffaretti, 2009b: 46–47). Each national central bank would be allocated an index quota equal to the sum of its imports and exports, averaged over the previous five years, and would be entitled to overdraw its clearing account by up to the value of its index account. If a deficit remained above one quarter of the index value for more than a year, the 'deficiency bank' would be allowed to borrow from the clearing account of a bank running a surplus, whilst the deficit nation would be entitled to devalue its exchange rate by up to 5 per cent per year. If the deficit exceeded half the index quota, this devaluation would be *required*, whilst outward movements of capital would be prohibited without the express permission of the governors of the central bank itself.

Meanwhile, surplus banks would be encouraged or, if the surplus balance exceeded 50 per cent of the index quota, required to introduce corrective measures. These would involve either currency appreciation, to the maximum of 5 per cent per annum, or easing the restrictions upon the outward flow of capital. At the year end, surplus balances still exceeding the value of the index quota would be transferred to the reserve fund of the central bank. In addition, surplus nations would be caused to transfer into the central bank's reserve fund 5 per cent of the annual excess above one quarter of its index quota, and 10 per cent above half the quota figure (Keynes, 1980a: 35–37). In essence, this imposed the equivalent of a rate of interest upon credit balances, in the attempt to provide a deterrent against the development of a persistent surplus position. This was intended to encourage creditors to expand their economic activity and thus avoid future charges (Lavoie, 2015: 5–7). In later drafts, this element was reluctantly dropped. However, it is proposed to retain it in the case of the Eurozone, as this element of the proposal would seem to have particular relevance to its particular circumstances (Keynes, 1980a: 96).

Utilisation of reserves to promote investment

Idle balances represent unused purchasing power which, in turn, prevents the maintenance of a level of aggregate demand sufficient to ensure full employment. In global terms, the reserves held by monetary authorities are equivalent to in excess of 12 per cent of world output at market exchange rates (Costabile, 2010: 7; Stiglitz and Greenwald, 2010: 8). Leaving these balances idle creates an opportunity cost, since these funds could have been invested in productive activity. Hence, the world economy is poorer and with a slower potential growth trajectory as a result (Stiglitz and Greenwald, 2010: 8, 12).

The ICU was designed to prevent the build-up of such excess reserves. It would do so by ensuring that such credit balances were recycled and utilised if holders were unwilling to do this themselves (Riese, 2008: 39; Whyman, 2015). Keynes expected that the threat of lost potential purchasing power would ensure that surplus nations used their otherwise idle balances to either prevent accumulation of idle balances in the first place, by boosting domestic demand, or through creating productive capacity abroad, through Foreign Direct Investment (FDI) or loans made to deficit nations. The point of the 'use it or lose it' clause was to prevent creditor nations from remaining passive and placing all adjustment burdens upon deficit nations (Keynes, 1980a: 49, 117). Essentially, the ICU proposal was designed to provide what Varoufakis (2015: 62) described as a "global surplus recycling mechanism".

Nevertheless, in the absence of creditor nation action, the ICU retained the ability to make use of any credit balances that surplus nations choose to remain idle, and recycle them through offering loans to deficit nations. It would therefore ensure the maintenance of a sufficient level of effective demand adequate to sustain full employment within the clearing union (Riese, 2008: 39). Hoarding would not be permitted. Moreover, there would be no cost associated with the recycling of these funds to the surplus nations, since they had chosen not to use these resources themselves. Hence, the ICU could invest these idle balances in much the same way as a domestic bank with savings accounts (Keynes, 1980a: 113). As a result, Kalecki and Schumacher (1943) concluded that the combination of an ICU and institutional investment office should be sufficient to provide sufficient short- and long-term lending to prevent unsustainable foreign exchange problems.

Exchange-rate adjustment

One key difference between the ICU and the existing European version of EMU, concerns the fact that the former envisages a *common* "currency union" (Keynes, 1980a: 44), within a system of fixed but adjustable exchange rates, rather than a *single* currency. The ICU was conceived as a means of supporting a fixed exchange rate system because this allowed for occasional readjustments in currency values to deal with persistent competitive problems that would otherwise need to be dealt with through internal devaluation – i.e. austerity measures and reductions in the social wage. Adjustments would be permitted if efficiency wages increased relative to wages abroad (Meltzer, 1983: 19; Keynes, 1980a: 274).

It is difficult to design a single currency regime that is optimal for all countries, or even for each individual nation on all occasions (Frankel, 1999: 2, 29). Consequently, whilst there are potential economic advantages in securing greater exchange-rate stability, in terms of providing more favourable conditions for the expansion of trade and to facilitate business investment, Keynes's preference was for a system of managed *but adjustable* exchange rates, due to his prioritisation of the achievement of domestic policy objectives to secure full employment (Smithin and Wolf, 1993: 369–371). Moreover, his preference was for national control over monetary policy, in order to maintain a low rate of interest (Keynes, 1980b: 16–19; Smithin and Wolf, 1993: 370). Given the well-established trade-offs between policy instruments and objectives, often termed the 'incompatible triangle', whereby fixed exchange-rates, independent monetary policy and the freedom of capital movements cannot be simultaneously achieved (Cooper, 2000: 295–297), Keynes opted for exchange rate stability, supported by restrictions upon the movement of capital (see Figure 2.2).

Economic integration does not, in any case, necessitate the introduction of a single currency, whether you define the process in terms of market convertibility (Vaubel, 1990: 936) or in terms of the creation of closer trade links between nations. Economic integration occurred between EU member states in its early years, with each member state having its own currency pegged within the Bretton Woods system of fixed but adjustable exchange rates. Similarly, it occurred between the USA and Canada more recently, despite both nations having free floating national currencies (Stiglitz, 2016: 45). There have, moreover, been many historical examples of establishing a common monetary standard, around which national currencies are fixed within a narrow band; the Gold Standard and the Bretton Woods system are the two most prominent examples (McKinnon, 1994: 337). Moreover, a common currency need not imply common banknotes. In the USA, for example, it is possible to identify the twelve Reserve Banks who issue currency. What matters is that each national or regional currency unit is fully convertible with each other at a rigidly fixed exchange rate and electronic payments would take place in the common currency (Cooper, 2000: 303).

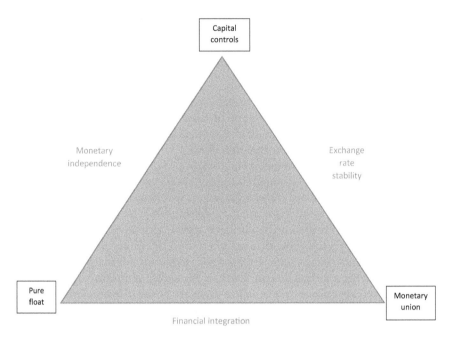

Figure 2.2 Policy trade-offs between monetary independence, exchange-rate stability and financial integration – 'the impossible trinity'

(Source: Figure adapted by the author from Frankel [1999: 8]).

There have, moreover, been a number of different proposals made to introduce common currency models to foster economic integration, whether in Asia (Mundell, 2003: 4) or Europe; the latter including proposals for parallel currencies (Vaubel, 1978), complementary currencies (Theret and Kalinowski, 2012) and dual currency models (Mazier and Valdecantos, 2015: 97). Of these, it is the latter that comes closest to the Keynes ICU proposal, since it would include adjustment of re-introduced national exchange rates (Mazier and Valdecantos, 2015: 98). However, this particular proposal is rather complex, involving the splitting the Eurozone into two segments, namely a 'Northern' and 'Southern' Euro area, which would seem to be unnecessary in a fully fledged ICU system, since any persistent shifts in international competitiveness could be rectified by adjusting each individual national currency peg as and when this became necessary.

The economic argument for having a single currency is far from compelling, with likely reductions in transaction costs being quite modest and the degree to which economic integration has been secured prior to the introduction of the single currency obviously reduces the scope for further integration gains post-introduction. A single currency does eliminate one form of risk to the economy, namely the possibility of a change in the exchange rate, but it does so at the cost of potential real currency misalignments (Stiglitz, 2016: 46, 50). Moreover, as was discussed in the previous chapter, the introduction of a single currency could encourage those nations with competitive advantage to specialise in certain industries, thereby reducing the diversification of production across the single currency zone and thereby increasing the risk of asymmetric external shocks. Once the single currency zone becomes unbalanced, history indicates that it can be difficult to eliminate in all but the long run (Varoufakis, 2015: 61).

Given the disadvantages of the single currency option, it is reasonable to question why it was chosen as the basis for EMU in Europe in the first place. The most plausible answer to this question is that the Delors Committee considered that it represented a more irrevocable option, in that the costs of dismantling the system (or for one or more participants to withdraw), would be far higher once national currencies had been abolished and replaced with the Euro (Mundell, 2003: 4). Thus, the very rigidity and inflexibility of the single currency that has been the cause of much economic damage over the past decade, was initially viewed by its advocates as providing greater stability to the single currency regime, if policy reversal had been made prohibitively costly.

This conclusion is questionable, of course, in that a single currency that proves to be unsustainable in the medium term may itself lack credibility (Vaubel, 1990: 942). Moreover, a common currency approach has a second advantage over a single currency, in that economic crisis in one participating member state would not threaten the stability of the entire currency zone. Instead, the nation could have its currency peg altered to better fit its new circumstances or, if that form of adjustment was deemed to be insufficient to solve certain deep-seated problems in their economy, that nation could withdraw from the mechanism, perhaps for a moderately short period, until it had satisfactorily resolved its problems (McKinnon, 1994: 355).

Issues arising from the Keynes Plan

Many of the initial reactions to the Keynes Plan are documented elsewhere (de Vegh, 1943; Horsefield, 1969; Keynes, 1980a; Riese, 2008). However, there were a number of issues, arising out of the Plan, identified as potentially problematic for the adoption and operation of the scheme.

The first relates to relations between ICU participants and non-members. Given that the ICU was devised as a means of resolving problems for the global economy, it would operate more smoothly if all nation states participated. However, this was always going to be unlikely. Consequently, the ICU would have to accommodate trade between member and non-member states. If non-ICU nations wished to trade with ICU member states – and there is a presumption that they would if they had an existing trade surplus with these nations – then they would need to establish an account with the ICU Clearing Bank. Ultimate balances would be cleared between central banks of member and non-member states alike, through ICU Clearing Bank accounts (Keynes, 1980a: 61–62). Nations generating a trade surplus with the ICU would hold a credit balance, and those with a trade deficit, a debit account, which they would have to settle through transfer of foreign exchange or other assets (Keynes, 1980a: 176, 223).

There is a question as to whether non-member states would wish to trade with the ICU, since they would be subject to the same rules as members but without influence. However, withdrawing from trade relationships with ICU member states would be damaging to non-participants. Nations running a trade deficit with ICU members could not maintain an overdraft facility, and hence would have to settle their accounts into the Clearing Bank using any previous bancor credits or utilising other financial securities. For nations running a surplus, if they chose to retain credit balances unused, there would be little practical difference, albeit that these would have to be held in bancor, rather than their own currencies, except that excess reserves would be recycled and used within the clearing union, thereby maintaining potential purchasing power in those nations buying exported goods from surplus nations. If, however, the surplus nations chose to use these balances themselves, they would be restricted to do so within the ICU economy and not withdrawn from the clearing union (Keynes, 1980a: 83, 112, 122).

A second, related point concerns the position of surplus nations within the ICU. As a voluntary system, from which nations can decline to participate or withdraw subject to one year's notice (and leaving any credit balances within the clearing union), surplus nations will necessarily require benefits of some kind to outweigh the costs related to the restrictions upon behaviour that the ICU would impose (Riddle, 1943: 15).

The most powerful argument relates to disquiet concerning the stability and long-term sustainability of present international payments arrangements. Historical evidence would seem to suggest that disproportionate loading of adjustment costs upon deficit nations has been a fundamental flaw in previous fixed currency systems (Keynes, 1980a: 27). Thus, surplus nations (i.e. Germany, Czech Republic) cannot continue to prosper, in the long term, by causing their trading partners (i.e. Greece, Italy, Spain, Portugal) to respond through deflation. Reduced demand, in deficit nations, reduces the exports of surplus nations unless they respond through their own internal deflation, thereby initiating a further beggar-thy-neighbour deflationary spiral. The ICU would provide a longer term sustainable solution to this dilemma for surplus nations (Keynes, 1980a: 276).

Surplus nations may, furthermore, benefit through any promotion of deeper economic integration, especially in relation to the completion of the single market, arising from the introduction of the ICU programme (Keynes, 1980a: 121). In addition, the ability of the ICU to prevent deflation and reductions in social wages across a large swathe of the Eurozone – undertaken in order to promote international competitiveness (due, in no small part, to persistent trade imbalances) – would promote the social solidarity across the EU which seems rather lacking at present.

A third issue is related to the first, in that nations are reluctant to surrender sovereignty in economic matters. Keynes (1942) dismissed this as necessitating no greater loss than might occur under a standard commercial treaty. However, his claim would appear to be a little disingenuous, as commercial contracts do not restrict what one party can do with the proceeds of the activity, in the way that the ICU would impose upon creditor nations. Indeed, he acknowledged that the post-war world would require a "greater surrender of sovereign rights" than had been accepted to that point (Keynes, 1980a: 57). Instead, he argued that the discipline inherent within the ICU system would be advantageous, since it encouraged nation states to reject "indiscipline, disorder and bad neighbourliness" which had so often operated to the general disadvantage of all nations concerned (Keynes, 1980a: 57–58). It, furthermore, implied the creation of a new instrument of economic leadership and economic governance, which could assist in the promotion of global economic development and macroeconomic management (de Vegh, 1943: 544, 547; Keynes, 1980a: 58–60, 90–92, 131–133).

A fourth issue arising from the ICU proposal, and one that Keynes identified as perhaps the most difficult issue to resolve, relates to the demarcation of rules and discretion in the design of the system (Keynes, 1980a: 73, 116–117). In his early drafts of the Plan, Keynes erred on the side of designing a rule-based system, capable of restraining economic indiscipline, whereas in later drafts, he softened this stance, due to peer feedback, in order to allow greater discretion for government policy to adapt to circumstances and take whatever measures were necessary at the time Keynes, 1980a: 48, 78). He noted the theoretical preference for rules, but that discretion is probably necessary to make the system work more effectively in practice (Keynes, 1980a: 97, 116). Indeed, he remained essentially undecided about the balance between rule and discretion, concluding that it might be finally determined after the scheme had been enacted for an initial experimental period of a few years (Keynes, 1980a: 117).

In terms of the choice of a supranational body which has the strength and authority to be able to manage an international monetary system, Davidson has suggested two alternatives. In the first, a closed, double-entry bookkeeping clearing institution might be sufficient to keep track of net international payment positions between participating trading nations, and monitor compliance with the mutually agreed rules intended to solve problems of persistent trade and payments imbalances (Davidson, 2009: 136–142). His second suggestion would be to utilise the format of a central bank, similar to the current European Central Bank (ECB), in order to take advantage of the acceptance and credibility associated with an existing format, albeit that it would have to embrace rather different objectives (Davidson, 1992: 8). At the minimum, this would require the ECB to enshrine payments balance as a core part of its mandate, but, additionally, to seek to operate the ICU to secure and maintain full employment within the Euro-ICU zone (Davidson, 1992; Arestis, 1999: 9). This would necessitate a radical reform in ECB structure, strategic objectives and its willingness to use a broader use of differential policy tools, before it would be an acceptable conduit.

A final issue concerns potential inflationary effects arising from the operation of the ICU. For example, Meltzer (1983: 19) claims that Keynes was aware of the possible inflationary bias of his scheme, due to an excess supply of money, but that this flaw was not addressed. He suggests that this may have been because the scheme was unlikely to be accepted by the American negotiators at the Bretton Woods summit. The argument is advanced that the ICU provides surplus nations with an incentive to expand their economy, rather than allow build-up of surpluses triggering an exchange-rate appreciation. If the economy was already operating at full employment, this would be inflationary. Similarly, persistent deficit nations would be expected to devalue, which would improve the competitiveness of their exports but also provide an expansionary effect. In combination, these two measures would provide a stimulus to economic activity across the ICU. If economies were already operating at full employment levels, then this would be inflationary.

This critique ignores two counter arguments. The first is that the ICU would act as a closed system, and so devaluation by one participating (deficit) nation would imply relative appreciation by another (surplus) nation. Thus, as the change in pegs stimulates one economy, with insufficient purchasing power due to its trade deficit, it deflates another which has potentially too much demand generated by its trade surplus.

The second argument is to consider the basic starting point which led to the development of the Keynes Plan in the first place, namely that the operation of the current international payments system – through asymmetric treatment of deficit and surplus nations, alongside the amassing of idle reserves – has a profound *deflationary* effect upon the global economy (Keynes, 1980a: 46–48, 60, 74–77, 112–113). The ICU was *supposed* to reverse this effect, thereby providing better global balance. Moreover, it would do so with no burden placed upon surplus nations (Keynes, 1980a: 112, 115). If this analysis is correct, then it is likely that the global economy would 'run hotter', with less wasted resources, and the varied evidence arising from Phillips Curve, NAIRU and other policy trade-off analysis, would indicate that inflationary pressures may arise at slightly less than full employment equilibrium. Nevertheless, even if this analysis is correct, this is more of a problem for the correct use of macroeconomic policy tools, rather than a justification to reject the ICU system.

Relevance to the EU in 2017

Having outlined the fundamental elements of the Keynes Plan, the relevance to the difficulties faced by the Eurozone should be obvious to the reader. The current asymmetry of economic development within the Eurozone, and the resulting internal imbalances, threaten to undermine the solidarity that underpins the European project (Bibow, 2007: 31). The experience of previous fixed exchange-rate regimes would suggest that loading the burden of adjustment upon weaker (deficit) nations, such as Greece or Portugal as at present, exacerbates tensions and facilitates political or popular opposition. Moreover, reliance upon export-led growth, to compensate for inadequate domestic levels of aggregate demand, depends upon external economies continuing to accept symmetrical trade deficits. Neither of these factors is likely to persist in the long term, and the Eurozone is not currently constructed to contribute towards the unwinding of imbalances, and thereby reducing the threat to its sustainability (Bibow, 2007: 34).

Were an ICU reform to be introduced, the asymmetric nature of the current Eurozone rescue plans, which dampen demand in already struggling member states and provide only temporary relief, could be exchanged for a system which would automatically ensure a *symmetric* rebalancing of the Eurozone. There would be fewer macro-precautionary reasons for holding idle reserves, with consequent loss of potential purchasing power within the Eurozone, as an ICU would facilitate a more expansive European economy, with fewer inherent trade-related tensions and lower perceptions of risks associated with deflationary policies necessitated by trade imbalances. Creditor nations would be encouraged to either increase the economic activity in their own economies, and thereby suck in more imports and reduce excess surplus balances or, if already at or near full employment, to spend these reserves in debtor nations, through direct investment (FDI) or the provision of foreign aid. Otherwise, the ICU would ensure that excess credit balances would be utilised, perhaps through a European Investment Foundation, as suggested by Arestis (1999: 9–10). Whatever the method chosen, the result should be the union experiencing a higher level of aggregate demand, as resources are not withdrawn as the result of a build-up of reserves or deflation imposed upon deficit nations, and thereby growth should rise and unemployment fall across participating member states.

One advantage that the EU has, over supporters of the original Keynes Plan in the 1940s, is that part of the infrastructure necessary for the operation of the scheme is already in place. The ECB already exists as an accepted supranational economic authority, and as such, this could form the basis for the clearing agency proposed by Keynes to manage the clearing union. Moreover, the Trans-European Automated Real-Time Gross Settlement Express Transfer System (TARGET2) clearing and settlement system that has been put in place in the Eurozone has several similarities with one important element of Keynes's proposals, in that it seeks to recycle idle national surpluses (Lavoie, 2015: 7). This meets part of the criteria of the ICU proposal but it fails to provide a satisfactory means of securing lasting adjustment in competitiveness, given that the current variant of EMU precludes adjustments in exchange rates, and thereby eventual adjustments will be considerably more painful for the economies concerned under the current model of EMU rather than the Keynesian ICU alternative (Cesaratto, 2013: 369–370).

The adoption of an ICU would, however, not be without significant difficulties. The most obvious criticism is that, once the single currency had been implemented, this would effectively close off alternative models of EMU, however attractive they may be in theory, "without passing through hell" in the transition from one model to another (Bellofiore, 2013: 509). This is a persuasive argument, and, indeed, echoes the point made by former Greek Finance Minister, Varoufakis (2016: 142), when he describes the model of EMU having created a "Hotel California" that it was impossible to leave.

It is possible to conceive of an 'ICU-lite' version of Keynes's proposals that could implement some of the key elements of the scheme, even within the constraints of the existing single currency. This could include measures to promote symmetric adjustment to trade imbalances, either through incentives for surplus nations to use idle balances, the introduction of some form of 'recycling mechanism', whereby savings generated through trade surpluses automatically lent to member states with trade deficits (Barba and De Vivo, 2013), or through exhortation to encourage surplus nations to increase their domestic demand (US Department of the Treasury, 2013: 3). It is even conceivable that a separate reserve currency (Euro-bancor) could be introduced alongside the Euro, to operate final clearing accounts between member states, protected by capital controls, and with a system of incentives designed to encourage the recycling of idle balances. Reform of the rules constraining fiscal policy could assist in stabilising the single currency, through the introduction of a variant of fiscal federalism, whilst reform to the ECB could allow it to become a true lender of last resort, which would provide further assistance to the Eurozone.

Unfortunately, even if this series of reforms were to be introduced, the net result would fall well short of the original Keynes Plan, because it would be focused upon attempting to stabilise a system but where, if individual countries developed a persistent trade imbalance, whether due to an internal or external shock, there is no simple means of restoring balance through currency realignment. Deprived of their ability to devaluate, Eurozone countries in crisis may become stuck in a demand-deficient, low-growth equilibrium. In the ICU proposal, whilst the symmetrical rebalancing facilitated via the ICU should reduce problems arising from large and persistent surpluses and deficits (Keynes, 1980a: 77), it was envisaged that any remaining fundamental trade imbalances were addressed through changes in exchange rates. Indeed, it has been argued that the re-introduction of Keynesian policies at the national level requires at least some ability to adjust the external value of the currency when this moves out of line with the requirements of securing internal balance (Smithin and Wolf, 1993: 367).

It would, in theory, be possible to impose the equivalent to a devaluation or revaluation upon all contracts and financial assets held in a given country of the Eurozone (Mazier and Valdecantos, 2015; Lavoie, 2015: 15). But this would require quite draconian powers to be adopted by the Commission or ECB in order to change the terms of a myriad contracts, negotiated between private companies and/or EU citizens, to create a similar effect to a rather straightforward managed change in relative currency values within the ICU. Thus, the full ICU variant would be a superior solution, since it would have a broader set of policy instruments, including currency realignment, with which to seek to restore persistent trade imbalances.

The full variant of the ICU would require the re-introduction of national currencies in order for rebalancing to work more effectively. In this scenario, each member of the Eurozone would possess their individual currency, and use the Euro as their international bank currency intended to resolve balance of payments. As credit or debit balances grew, the option of encouraged or enforced currency revaluation and devaluation would be possible, thereby securing a quicker and more effective symmetric rebalancing of the clearing union than could be accomplished through the alternative plethora of incentives, outlined in the previous paragraph. The 'ICU-full' version, therefore, would incorporate all of the main aspects of the original Keynes Plan, namely symmetric rebalancing, a closed system of payments combined with capital controls, and the combination of the bank currency with the retention of national currencies, thereby enabling exchange-rate revision to reflect changes in competitiveness.

The argument that shifting to a common currency approach would require wholesale and potentially disruptive change to the entire EMU model, including its supportive infrastructure, is, therefore, of course correct. Yet, a similarly disruptive set of reforms would be required under any 'ICU-lite' proposals. Any Keynesian reform to the current variant of EMU, for it to be meaningful, would necessitate the wholesale redesign of the model, thereby incurring a significant level of unavoidable disruption during the transition period. Consequently, given the need to resolve the fundamental flaws lying at the heart of the current model of EMU, and the apparent necessity for the neo monetarist logic to impose a harsh and ultimately defeatist regime of austerity upon deficit member states, it can be advanced that this is precisely the correct time for the Eurozone partners to consider a different way of achieving the same ends. Rather than trying to improve a flawed model of EMU, this would be a good point in time to replace it with an approach that is likely to be more sustainable in the long run.

Another potential difficulty with the practical implementation of the ICU proposal relates to the current state of the international finance system. Compared to the more managed economies characterising the period in which Keynes developed his ideas, contemporary central banks are far less in control of the creation of credit and the establishment of interest rates (Arestis, 1999: 9). Liberalisation and the subsequent internationalisation of financial markets have combined to weaken the control of central banks (Fiorentini and Montani, 2010: E-27). Indeed, many argue that the free circulation of capital is an irreversible process (Fiorentini and Montani, 2010: E-27).

The problem with this argument is that, independent of any shift towards an ICU model of EMU, the necessity to regulate financial capital has been amply demonstrated by the experience of the past few decades and especially in relation to the impact of the recent global financial crisis. Even before this event, Cartapanis and Herland (2002: 273–274) were already observing that "rarely in the course of history had the international financial markets experienced such violent adjustments as those that have taken place in recent years". The IMF, for example, had documented 124 separate systemic banking crises that had occurred between the demise of Bretton Woods and the start of the 2008 global financial crisis (Laeven and Valencia, 2008: 5). One significant factor underpinning this increase in financial volatility has been the liberalisation of capital movements (Cartapanis and Herland, 2002: 274). Consequently, re-regulation of international financial capital movements would appear overdue. The fact that this is problematic is due, in large part, to the hegemonic dominance of neo-classical orthodoxy, which does not seem to have been as fatally wounded by the crisis as might have been anticipated. Thus, whilst such reforms would appear to be necessary to reduce volatility in financial markets and to strengthen the efficiency of macroeconomic policy interventions, it is quite plausible that the introduction of an ICU in Europe would face hostile market movements during the transition period.

Capital restrictions would additionally, at least superficially, appear to conflict with the 'four freedoms' enshrined in the Treaty of Rome; one of which being the freedom of movement of capital. The clearing union would have, at its heart, restrictions upon the convertibility of currencies into Euro-bancor and the regulation of the supranational clearing agency authority of all capital movements not related directly to trade or long-term productive investment. This would necessarily constrain the freedom of movement of capital. However, the EU has never been absolutist in its adherence to these principles, when they conflict with other objectives. For example, discussions regarding the advisability of introducing a form of Tobin tax (1978), to prevent short-term speculative financial transactions from undermining economic stability, would imply that the principle of freedom of movement of capital is not sacrosanct. Moreover, the ICU proposal would encourage the expansion of international trade in goods and services, alongside long-term productive investment, so it would only be short-term capital movements which would be severely curtailed. This would not hamper the completion of the European single internal market and, indeed, may facilitate its progress.

Fundamental change of theoretical underpinning for the ECB would, moreover, be required in addition to a radical revision of its objectives. Thus, the narrow focus upon low inflation would need to be superseded by the task of managing the clearing union and, as a consequence, to prioritise the facilitation of full employment across the union. This is incompatible with a theoretical adherence to economic orthodoxy, with a neo-liberal flavour, and hence the ECB and its officers would need to accept the tenants of Keynesian theory. This will prove problematic, given the dominance of orthodox economic perspectives in the finance sector and, albeit to a lesser extent, to academia; the two areas from which potential ECB officials might be drawn. Nevertheless, given the importance of the new institution for the success of the new policy orientation, sufficient candidates could be found amongst the minority heterodox economist communities.

The final problem for the EU, in adopting an ICU proposal, is quite simply that the EU Commission and Eurozone participants would need to acknowledge that the present form of EMU is fatally flawed – and neither politicians nor economists appear to welcome having to admit previous mistakes. For some, it might be that they are 'true believers' in the new monetarist, neo-liberal economic foundations of the current model of EMU, and therefore do not recognise the validity of an alternative approach. For others, it may be because the re-introduction of national exchange rates might appear to be a reversal of previous steps to deepen European economic integration, even if an ICU version might actually secure a more sustainable long-term future. For yet others it might be because they are concerned with the consequences of short-term economic disruption, during a transition period moving from a single to a common currency regime, even if the latter were to deliver superior performance over the medium to longer term. Thus, it is likely that any shift towards a common currency solution will require two elements; first, the demonstration of the feasibility and desirability of the alternative approach, to which this book will hopefully make a small contribution, but second, a political struggle of some kind to realise this more progressive alternative.

Notes

1 'Europa "Before the ESM"' (European Stability Mechanism). www.efsf.europa.eu/about/index.htm (accessed 22 November 2017); http://ec.europa.eu/economy_finance/eu_borrower/efsm/index_en.htm; http://ec.europa.eu/economy_finance/publications/giovannini/giovannini081100en.pdf.
2 Interviewed on the BBC Radio 4 programme 'Inside the IMF', broadcast in December 2010, and available via: www.bbc.co.uk/programmes/b00wldvt. The ideas were further discussed in a blog by the interviewer, Stephanie Flanders, available via: www.bbc.co.uk/blogs/thereporters/stephanieflanders/2010/12/the_imf_according_to_keynes.html.

Bibliography

Alves, A.J., Ferrari Jr, F. and De Paula, L.F.R. (1999), 'The Post Keynesian Critique of Conventional Currency Crisis Models and Davidson's Proposal to Reform the International Monetary System', *Journal of Post Keynesian Economics*, 22(2): 207–225.

Arestis, P. (1999), 'The Independent European Central Bank: Keynesian Alternatives', *Levy Economics Institute Working Paper* No. 274.

Arestis, P. and Sawyer, M. (2000), 'Deflationary Consequences of the Single Currency', in Baimbridge, M., Burkitt, B. and Whyman, P.B. (Eds.), *The Impact of the Euro: Debating Britain's Future*, Macmillan, London.

Baimbridge, M., Burkitt, B. and Whyman, P.B. (2012), 'The Eurozone as a Flawed Currency Area', *Political Quarterly*, 83(1): 96–107.

Barba, A. and De Vivo, G. (2013), 'Flawed Currency Areas and Viable Currency Areas: External Imbalances and Public Finance in the Time of the Euro', *Contributions to Political Economy*, 32(1): 73–96.

Bayoumi, T. and Eichengreen, B. (1993), 'Shocking Aspects of European Monetary Integration', in Torres, F. and Giavazzi, F. (Eds.), *Adjustment and Growth in the European Monetary Union*, Cambridge University Press, Cambridge, 193–229.

Bellofiore, R. (2013), 'Two or Three Things I Know about Her: Europe in the Global Crisis and Heterodox Economics', *Cambridge Journal of Economics*, 37(3): 497–512.

Bibow, J. (2007), 'Global Imbalances, Bretton Woods II and Euroland's Role in All This', *Levy Economics Institute Working Paper* No. 486.

Bibow, J. (2010), 'Bretton Woods 2 Is Dead, Long Live Bretton Woods 3?', *Levy Economics Institute Working Paper* No. 597.

Burkitt, B., Baimbridge, M. and Whyman, P. (1996), *There is an Alternative*, Nelson & Pollard, Oxford.

Cartapanis, A. and Herland, M. (2002), 'The Reconstruction of the International Financial Architecture: Keynes' Revenge?', *Review of International Political Economy*, 9(2): 271–297.

Cesaratto, S. (2013), 'The Implications of TARGET2 in the European Balance of Payments Crisis and Beyond', *European Journal of Economics and Economic Policies: Intervention*, 10(3): 359–382.

Cooper, R.N. (2000), 'Toward a Common Currency?', *International Finance*, 3(2): 287–308.

Costabile, L. (2010), 'The International Circuit of Key Currencies and the Global Crisis: Is There Scope for Reform?', *PERI Working Paper* No. 220.

D'Arista, J. (2003), 'Reforming the Privatised International Monetary and Financial Archi-tecture', in Mullineux, A.W. and Murinde, V. (Eds.), *Handbook of International Banking*, Edward Elgar, Cheltenham, 721–750.

De Grauwe, P. and Vanhaverbeke, W. (1993), 'Is Europe an Optimum Currency Area?', in Masson, P.R. and Taylor, M.P. (Eds.), *Policy Issues in the Operation of Currency Unions*, Cam-bridge University Press, Cambridge, 111–129.

Davidson, P. (1982), *International Money and the Real World*, Macmillan, London.

Davidson, P. (1992), 'Reforming the World's Money', *Journal of Post Keynesian Economics*, 15(2): 153–179.

Davidson, P. (1994), *Post Keynesian Macroeconomic Theory*, Edward Elgar, Aldershot.

Davidson, P. (2009), *The Keynes Solution: The Path to Global Economic Prosperity*, Palgrave, London.

De Grauwe, P. (2013), 'Design Failures in the Eurozone: Can They Be Fixed?', *Euro-pean Economy Economics Papers*, No. 491, European Commission, Brussels. Available via: http://ec.europa.eu/economy_finance/publications/economic_paper/2013/pdf/ecp491_en.pdf.

Degryse, C. (2012), 'The New Economic Governance', *ETUI Working Paper* No. 14.

de Vegh, I. (1943), 'The International Clearing Union', *American Economic Review*, 33(3): 534–556.

Eichengreen, B. (1992), 'Is Europe an Optimum Currency Area?', in Borner, S. and Grubel, H. (Eds.), *The European Community after 1992: Perspectives from the Outside*, Macmillan, London, 138–161.

EU Commission (2011), *Green Paper on the Feasibility of Introducing Stability Bonds* [COM 818], European Commission, Brussels.

Fiorentini, R. and Montani, G. (2010), 'Global Imbalances and the Transition to a Symmetric World Monetary Order', *Perspectives on Federalism*, 2(1): E1–E42.

Frankel, J.A. (1999), 'No Single Currency Regime is Right for All Countries or at All Times', *NBER Working Paper* No. 7338. Available via: http://www.nber.org/papers/w7338.

Horsefield, J.K. (1969), *The International Monetary Fund 1945–1965 – Volume 3: Documents*, International Monetary Fund, Washington, DC.

Kalecki, M. (1946), 'Multilateralism and Full Employment', *Canadian Journal of Economics and Political Science*, 12: 322–327.

Kalecki, M. and Schumacher, E.F. (1943), 'International Clearing and Long-Term Lending', *Bulletin of the Oxford Institute of Statistics*, 5(Supplement): 29–33.

Keynes, J.M. (1923), *A Tract on Monetary Reform*, Macmillan, London.

Keynes, J.M. (1930), *A Treatise on Money: The Applied Theory of Money*, reproduced in Johnson, E. and Moggridge, D. (Eds.) (1978), *The Collected Writings of John Maynard Keynes*, Volume 6, Royal Economic Society and Cambridge University Press, Cambridge.

Keynes, J.M. (1933), *The Means to Prosperity*, Macmillan, London.

Keynes, J.M. (1936), *The General Theory of Employment, Interest and Money*, Macmillan, Basingstoke, 1973 edition.

Keynes, J.M. (1942), 'Proposals for an International Currency (or Clearing) Union: Fourth Draft of the "Keynes Plan"', reproduced in Horsefield, J.K. (1969), *The International Monetary Fund 1945–1965 – Volume 3: Documents*, International Monetary Fund, Washington, DC, 3–36.

Keynes, J.M. (1980a), 'Activities 1940–1944: Shaping the Post-War World – The Clearing Union', In Moggridge, D. (Ed.), *The Collected Writings of John Maynard Keynes*, Macmillan, London.

Keynes, J.M. (1980b), 'Activities 1941–1946: Shaping the Post-War World – Breton Woods and Reparations', In Moggridge, D. (Ed.), *The Collected Writings of John Maynard Keynes*, Macmillan, London. Krugman, P. (1999), *The Return of Depression Economics*, Penguin, London, revised 2000 edition.

Laeven, L. and Valencia, F. (2008), 'Systematic Banking Crises: A New Database', *International Monetary Fund Working Paper* No. 08/224.

Laski, K. and Podkaminer, L. (2012), 'The Basic Paradigms of EU Economic Policy-making Need to be Changed', *Cambridge Journal of Economics*, 36(1): 253–270.

Lavoie, M. (2015), 'The Eurozone: Similarities to and Differences From Keynes's Plan', *International Journal of Political Economy*, 44(1): 3–17.

Mazier, J. and Valdecantos, S. (2015), 'A Multi Speed Europe – Is It Viable? A Stock-Flow Consistent Approach', *European Journal of Economics and Economic Policies: Intervention*, 12(1): 93–112.

McKinnon, R.I. (1994), 'Common Monetary Standard or a Common Currency for Europe? Fiscal Lessons From the United States', *Scottish Journal of Political Economy*, 41(4): 337–357.

Meltzer, A.H. (1983), 'Keynes on Monetary Reform and International Economic Order', Paper presented at the *5th Henry Thornton Lecture*, 3 October, City University Business School, London. Available at: http://repository.cmu.edu/tepper/796/.

Moran, T.H., Graham, E. and Blomström, M. (Eds.) (2005), *Does Foreign Direct Investment Promote Development?* Institute for International Economics, Washington, DC, 23–44.

Mundell, R. (2003), 'Prospects for an Asian Currency Area', *Journal of Asian Economics*, 14(1): 1–10.

Piffaretti, N.F. (2009a), 'Reshaping the International Monetary Architecture: Lessons From Keynes' Plan', *World Bank Policy Research Working Paper* No. 5034.

Piffaretti, N.F. (2009b), 'Reshaping the International Monetary Architecture: Lessons From Keynes' Plan', *Banks and Bank Systems*, 4(1): 45–54.

Richardson, D.R. (1985), 'On Proposals for a Clearing Union', *Journal of Post Keynesian Economics*, 8(1): 14–27.

Riddle, J.H. (1943), *British and American Plans for International Currency Stabilisation*, National Bureau for Economic Research, Cambridge MA. Out of print edition, available via: www.nber.org/chapters/c4632.pdf.

Riese, M. (2008), *Reforming the Global Financial Architecture: A Comparison of Different Proposals*. Available via: www.singleglobalcurrency.org/documents/DAReformingtheGlobalFinancialArchitecturehyper.pdf.

Schiaffino, P. (2013), 'A Comment on the European Central Bank v's the Keynes Solution', *Journal of Post Keynesian Economics*, 35(3): 457–462.

Skidelsky, R. (2000), *John Maynard Keynes: Fighting for Britain, 1937–1946 v.3: Fighting for Britain, 1937–1946 – Vol 3*, Macmillan, London.

Skidelsky, R. (2005), 'Keynes, Globalisation and the Bretton Woods Institutions in the Light of Changing Ideas About Markets' *World Economics*, 6(1): 5–30.

Smithin, J. and Wolf, B.M. (1993), 'What Would Be a "Keynesian" Approach to Currency and Exchange Rate Issues?', *Review of Political Economy*, 5(3): 365–383.

Steil, B. (2013), *The Battle of Bretton Woods: John Maynard Keynes, Harry Dexter White, and the Making of a New World Order*, Princeton University Press, Princeton, NJ.

Stiglitz, J.A. (2016), *The Euro and Its Threat to the Future of Europe*, Allen Lane, London.

Stiglitz, J.E. and Greenwald, B. (2003), *Towards a New Paradigm in Monetary Economics*, Cambridge University Press, Cambridge.

Stiglitz, J.E. and Greenwald, B. (2010), 'Towards a New Global Reserve System', *Journal of Globalisation and Development*, 1(2): 1–24.

Theret, B. and Kalinowski, W. (2012), *The Euro as Common Money Not a Single Currency: A Plea for a European Monetary Federalism*, Veblaen Institute for Economic Reforms, Paris. Available via: www.cepn-paris13.fr/epog/wp-content/uploads/2015/09/THERET_a_plea_for_a_european_monetary_federalism.pdf.

Tobin, J. (1978), 'A Proposal for International Monetary Reform', *Eastern Economic Journal*, 4(3–4): 153–159.

US Department of the Treasury (2013), *Report to Congress on International Economic and Exchange Rate Policies*, US Department of the Treasury, Washington, DC. Available via: http://www.treasury.gov/resource-center/international/exchange-rate-policies/Documents/2013-10-30_FULL%20FX%20REPORT_FINAL.pdf.

Varoufakis, Y. (2015), *The Global Minotaur*, Zed Books, London.

Varoufakis, Y. (2016), *And the Weak Suffer What They Must?: Europe, Austerity and the Threat to Global Stability*, The Global Minotaur, Penguin-Random House, London.

Vaubel, R. (1978), *Strategies for Currency Unification: The Economics of Currency Competition and the Case for a European Parallel Currency*, Mohr, Turbingen.

Vaubel, R. (1990), 'Currency Competition and European Monetary Integration', *Economic Journal*, 100(402): 936–946.

Whyman, P.B. (2015), 'Keynes and the International Clearing Union: A Possible Model for Eurozone Reform?', *Journal of Common Market Studies*, 53(2): 399–415.

3 Monetary policy in the Keynesian EMU

[O]ur problem is not a human problem of muscles and endurance. It is not an engineering problem or an agricultural problem. It is not even a business problem, if we mean by business those calculations and dispositions and organising acts by which individual entrepreneurs can better themselves. Nor is it a banking problem, if we mean by banking those principles and methods of shrewd judgement by which lasting connections are fostered and unfortunate commitments avoided. On the contrary, it is, in the strictest sense, an economic problem, or, to express it better, as suggesting a blend of economic theory with the art of statesmanship, a problem of Political Economy.

(Keynes, 1933: 5–6)

Introduction

The current neo-liberal model of EMU has had a substantial impact upon monetary policy and financial regulation within the Eurozone. This is because the introduction of a single currency requires all participants to cede their monetary sovereignty to a supranational body, in this case the European Central Bank (ECB), which operates monetary policy for the whole of the Eurozone rather than being tailored to the specific needs of individual nations. As a result, there is always the risk that monetary policy will be too loose for certain member states and too tight for others. However, since the focus of the ECB is on the Eurozone as a whole, policy should focus upon the requirements of the average needs of all participants.

In addition, new monetarist economic thought underpins most features of the rules and institutions established for the operation of the Eurozone monetary policy. This includes the design of the ECB, the objectives established for it to pursue, the limitations to its ability to act as a lender of last resort, together with its ability to influence other aspects of EU macroeconomics such as fiscal policy and developments in social and labour policy. The net result has been a significant shift in the macroeconomic stance of many single currency participants towards a more orthodox or neo-liberal stance. However, it is this very theoretical underpinning of Eurozone monetary policy that has been found wanting in a number of key respects, during the recent financial and economic crises.

This chapter outlines certain key elements of the existing management of monetary policy within the current model of EMU, before contrasting this with how an alternative approach to monetary policy would operate under the common currency (ICU) version of EMU outlined in the previous chapter. This chapter, furthermore, seeks to highlight how certain features of the current system would need substantive reform. In particular, the ECB would need to be reconstituted as the primary agent capable of pursuing its new responsibilities in managing the ICU and co-ordinating monetary policy in such a way as to maintain full employment and adequate rates of growth across the ICU zone.

The current monetary policy model

The economic theory underpinning the current neo-liberal approach to monetary policy is threefold:

1   Adoption of the supply-determined rate of unemployment understanding of the economy – implying little or no room for active government macroeconomic management;
2   Acceptance of the time inconsistency problem, derived from assumptions of rational expectations – emphasising the importance of building anti-inflation credibility;
3   Central bank independence – intended to pursue monetary credibility and insulate monetary policy decisions from political influence.

The first element of the current approach to monetary policy draws upon the expectations-augmented, vertical long-run Phillips Curve, first developed by Friedman (1968) and Phelps (1968). This is, in turn, based upon a neo-classical view of the labour market, where rational self-maximising individuals choose how much time to work depending upon the prevailing real wages rate. Government intervention to increase employment, under this set of neo-classical assumptions, will ultimately prove futile, since any increase in nominal wages which may be expected to attract more individuals to increase their labour market participation will be offset by an increase in inflation. Thus, any attempt to reduce unemployment below the long-run equilibrium 'natural rate' will ultimately end in failure (Friedman, 1968: 8). Assuming that the market economy is essentially efficient, and will tend towards producing pricing decisions that will clear each individual market, Say's Law suggests that it will tend towards full employment of all resources in the economy. Hence, there is no role for the type of active macroeconomic management advocated by Keynesians, as supply factors determine economic fundamentals, and demand adjusts to this reality.

The time inconsistency problem builds upon this supposed insight, in that economic actors remain suspicious of governments seeking to use their informational advantage over firms and workers to manipulate economic policy for their short-term advantage (Lucas, 1976; Kyland and Prescott, 1977). This argument is essentially a variant of public choice theory, which suggests that politicians will seek to maximise their own utility at the expense of the national interest, by manipulating economic instruments to maximise their chances of re-election (Nordhaus, 1975; Cukierman, 1994: 1443). Accordingly, if it is assumed that economic actors possess rational expectations, they will be able to anticipate that government might undertake such behaviour and accordingly incorporate the expected higher rate of inflation into their pricing schedules or nominal wage demands. Thus, should government be tempted to attempt to stimulate the economy, monetary surprise would not occur and employment would remain static, albeit that the natural or equilibrium rate of unemployment now occurred at a higher rate of inflation. Thus, not only is policy activism ineffective, but it creates economic damage through increasing the rate of inflation, which is itself costly to economic actors.

The solution to this would be for the economic authorities to pre-commit that they would not attempt to 'surprise' other economic actors with such behaviour (Barro and Gordon, 1983). However, the difficulty here is getting economic actors to trust the government and other policymakers. To the extent that monetary authorities can build up an anti-inflationary reputation, economic actors will not need to build in a high risk premium into their activities because it is less likely that they will be surprised by unanticipated inflation or currency devaluation. The Maastricht convergence criteria and the Stability and Growth Pact may both be considered to be examples of this attempt to secure policy credibility (Clift, 2001: 64; Recio and Roca, 1998: 143). The difficulty here is that monetary authorities may not be trusted unless this pre-commitment was enshrined in a rule-based system that would be difficult for policymakers to change (Friedman, 1960, 1968, 1972: 227), or else policy would be devolved to an economic agency with greater credibility to pursue these policy rules.

Creating an operationally independent 'conservative' central bank is advanced as a means to secure a lower rate of inflation, in the medium to long term, than would otherwise prove possible with monetary policy remaining under a variant of political control (Rogoff, 1985; Alesina, 1989). To the extent that this is an accurate assertion, then an independent central bank would provide a superior institutional setting to control inflation. Moreover, if the hypotheses of supply-determined employment and rational expectations are proven to be correct, then the independent central bank would be able to do so with little or no cost in terms of increasing unemployment and slowing economic growth (Barro and Gordon, 1983; Grilli et al., 1991). Consequently, according to this viewpoint, long-term economic efficiency requires the removal of monetary policy from the sphere of democratically accountable politics. Such a move will also enhance the credibility of declared anti-inflationary strategies.

This set of neo-liberal economic perspectives informed much of the design of the current version of EMU. The newly established European Central Bank (ECB) drew much of its inspiration from the former Bundesbank, with its statutes being framed to create the most independent of all major central banks (Alesina and Grilli, 1991; Jabko, 1999). The ECB was established under the 1991 Maastricht Treaty (EU Commission, 1992), where Article 107 states that:

> When exercising the powers and carrying out the tasks and duties con-ferred upon them by this Treaty and the Statute of the ESCB, neither the ECB, nor a national central bank, nor any member of their decision-making bodies shall seek or take instructions from Community institutions or bodies, from any Government of a Member State or from any other body. The Community institutions and bodies and the governments of the Member States undertake to respect this principle and not to seek to influ-ence the members of the decision-making bodies of the ECB and of the national central banks in the performance of their tasks.

Eagerness on the part of many EU nation states to participate in EMU neces-sitated an acceptance of the principle of central bank autonomy from all gov-ernment influence and control, to the extent that Issing (2002: 9), former lead economist and board member for the European Central Bank, felt able to claim that:

> There is today a broad consensus that stable money is too important to be left to the day-to-day political process . . . it makes sense for society to create an independent institution that stands above the fray of day-to-day politics and can pursue this objective [price stability] with minimum distraction.

Article 127(1) of the Treaty on the Functioning of the European Union (TFEU) states that the primary objective of the ECB is to maintain price stability; pro-viding assistance to other macroeconomic objectives are relegated to being of secondary importance (ECB, 2011: 14). Price stability, for the benefit of the ECB, is defined as an inflation rate below 2 per cent, as calculated according to the Harmonised Index of Consumer Prices (HICP) method (ECB, 2011: 64). The justification for this goal prioritisation is based upon the principle of the long-run neutrality of money, which leaves real income and employment levels in the long run to be determined by supply-side factors (ECB, 2011: 55–56). In other words, the ECB strategy rests firmly upon the new monetarist or neo-liberal approach outlined above.

To realise this objective, the ECB undertakes a combination of signalling (to influence inflation expectations), open market operations (to influence short-term market interest rates) and by managing the supply of liquidity in the financial system through refinancing operations (ECB, 2011: 62–63, 77–78, 93; Micosso, 2015: 3–4). This is a form of inflation targeting (Bernanke et al., 1999), which is intended to use monetary policy instruments to reduce output volatility by guiding it to its supply-determined 'natural' level (Taylor, 1993). However, the ECB approach deviates from a typical inflation targeting strategy in that it adopts a medium-term reference point and, whilst there is no formal targeting of monetary aggregates, it does monitor the growth of the money supply (primarily M3), and 'leans into the wind' by targeting what it regards as excessive growth in such aggregates (Issing et al., 2001: 82–86; Micosso, 2015: 5). The development of low-inflation credibility is perceived as a key goal by the ECB, in that it assists its signalling and expectations-influencing stratagems (Issing et al., 2001: 45).

Critique

The foundations upon which the ECB was constructed are, however, problematic for a number of reasons.

The first is that the money supply is not *exogenous* but *endogenous*, in so far as it is largely created by the banking sector and monetary aggregates cannot be adequately controlled by the monetary authorities. From the Keynesian perspective, causation runs from nominal income to the demand for money to the stock of money, as the availability of loans facilitates the expansion of investment, which leads to an expansion of savings and bank deposits. Thus, money supply does not *cause* inflation, but rather rising prices lead to a commensurate rise in the money supply (Arestis and Sawyer, 2004: 107–109).

Inflation originates from pressures in the *real* economy, whether due to capacity constraints or distributional conflict (Arestis et al., 2001). Firms set prices as a mark-up over average costs, the level of which is affected by factors such as the firm's market power and the buoyancy of demand in the economy; inflation occurs when demand exceeds productive capacity and firms face rising unit costs. Inflation is additionally influenced by the size and composition of the capital stock, as the larger the productive capital stock in the industry, the larger the number of employees and higher the real wage that should be compatible with a low level of inflation (Arestis and Sawyer, 2004). Since investment and the degree of capital utilisation are themselves both influenced by the state of expectations in the economy and the level of aggregate demand (Keynes, 1936: 135–141; Kalecki, 1971; Arestis, 1989: 614; Caporaso and Levine, 1992: 107), monetary policy can influence investment and the real economy, and thereby inflation.

Second, the supply-side determined long-run equilibrium rate of unemployment hypothesis has weak theoretical and empirical foundations. Keynesian monetary theory is based upon the proposition of *non-neutrality of money*. Indeed, this is one of the key areas of dispute between Keynesian and monetarist schools of thought. Keynes considered money to influence real variables through its impact upon the motives and decisions made by economic actors. Aggregate demand influences the real economy through its impact upon, and in turn is influenced by, the rate of investment, which in turn changes the stock of capital and thereby effects productive capacity. Thus, employment is determined in the product market by the aggregate demand for output.

The hysteresis theory builds upon this theoretical insight by noting that future unemployment depends upon the actual history or path of unemployment, meaning that it is *path-dependent*. This means that any equilibrium rate is only a temporary phenomenon, since current unemployment remains a significant factor determining future rates – a concept tantamount to replacing the concept of an equilibrium rate with a disequilibrium analysis. This supports the point made by Keynes that "there is no unique long-period position of equilibrium equally valid regardless of the character of the policy of the monetary authority" (Keynes, 1979: 55). This insight justifies policy activism to reduce actual unemployment beneath the prevailing equilibrium rate because, by so doing, it will enable that equilibrium rate to decline itself in the future (Blanchard and Summers, 1988). In essence, reducing unemployment in time period one will have the effect of lowering equilibrium unemployment in time period two. Thus, active monetary policy can facilitate an increase in aggregate demand, through reducing interest rates (or otherwise), thereby increasing output and potentially influencing growth rates, through negating hysteresis and encouraging the principle of cumulative causation. Essentially, "the problem of unemployment is ultimately one of investment" (Rowthorn, 1995: 38).

Third, the theory of rational expectations is based upon a number of unrealistic assumptions, including downplaying the importance of asymmetries of information and the fact that uncertainty is not the same as risk. The fact that asymmetric information exists suggests that economic actors make decisions with imperfect information and hence assumptions of rational behaviour leading to optimal outcomes becomes difficult to justify. Under these conditions, "unfettered markets, rampant with conflicts of interest, can lead to inefficiency" (Stiglitz, 2003: 152). In addition, the rational expectations hypothesis seems to confuse the concepts of uncertainty and risk. For the latter, it is possible for rational decision makers to examine time series data, develop a set of probabilities based upon past performance, which can be used to forecast future events with a degree of accuracy, and upon this analysis, to make fairly accurate decisions. Uncertainty is different. It means that certain variables or future events are not quantifiable in this way, and therefore economic actors must make decisions without the benefit of reasonably accurate future forecasts. Amidst conditions of uncertainty, economic actors not surprisingly can find it difficult to make consistent decisions and this may result in decisions taken according to volatile herd behaviour or what Keynes described as 'animal spirits' (Keynes, 1936: 155; Kahneman et al., 1982; Bell et al., 1988; Davidson, 1995; Lawson, 1995: 93–98; Galbraith, 1997; Stiglitz, 2003: 151–153; Shafir, 2004).

Fourth, there is a paucity of convincing theoretical or rigorous empirical evidence to support the case for central bank independence (Carvalho, 1995: 161; Cornwall and Cornwall, 1998: 63; Stiglitz, 2002: 45; Bibow, 2010: 3). Whilst a number of studies found a statistical relationship between low levels of inflation and the degree of central bank independence (Alesina, 1988; Cukierman, 1992; Alesina and Summers, 1993), this statistical relationship collapses once developing and transition countries are included in the analysis (Cukierman, 1992; Hillman, 1999). Furthermore, whilst the IMF (1996: 129) found a close inverse relationship between inflation and an index of central bank independence during the 1970s and 1980s, it found no such relationship during the 1960s and 1990s. Thus, it would appear that the oft-mentioned link between central bank independence and price stability depends upon the selection of the time series used in the calculations and, as such, can hardly be regarded as proven.

There is, moreover, evidence that central bank autonomy may result in lower and more volatile rates of economic growth, with deeper recessions and a higher sacrifice ratio of output lost associated with a reduction in inflation (Debelle and Fischer, 1994; Posen, 1995; Fischer, 1996; Jordan, 1997, 1999). 'Conservative' central bankers are likely to have an asymmetric reaction function when responding to problems of inflation and unemployment; being far more likely to react quickly and decisively to deal with the former rather than the latter. Thus, a greater stabilisation of prices would only arise at the expense of a greater instability of output and employment, resulting in a deadweight loss caused by sub-optimal output stabilisation (Rogoff, 1985; Bibow, 2004: 564). Thus, suggestions that independent, conservative central bankers can reduce the costs of disinflation can be dismissed as the 'power of wishful thinking' (Blinder, 1998: 63).

This is not to suggest that monetary authorities established to be functionally independent from government are inevitably conservative. Indeed, Keynes (1930: 243) himself advocated a form of central bank independence. However, the important point to note is that he was concerned only with operational independence, in order to enable an independent monetary agency with the freedom to use its discretion in the implementation and timing of monetary policy. However, the objectives of this agency would be determined by government and would therefore be democratically accountable. In his later work, such as *The General Theory*, the emphasis was more upon the importance of the co-ordination between fiscal and monetary policy, to prevent policy conflict becoming a source of instability (Bibow, 2009: 144). Nevertheless, it would seem to be a reasonable conclusion that Keynes would have supported the concept of an operationally independent central bank as long as it pursued policies intended to promote full employment and economic growth in addition to maintaining a low rate of inflation and securing financial stability.

Finally, empirical studies have found little evidence to suggest the existence of an optimal rate of inflation, which facilitates an optimal rate of growth (Akerlof et al., 1996; Sepehri and Moshiri, 2004: 191). Indeed, it would seem that inflation-targeting nations fared better in terms of inflation, output and employment, than other OECD (Organisation for Economic Co-operation and Development) countries pursuing other forms of monetary policy during the last decade (Ball and Sheridan, 2003).

The result of the problems inherent within the new monetarist theoretical framework, upon which the model of EMU and its accompanying supportive institutions were founded, is that the ECB was "flawed at birth" (Stiglitz, 2016: 146–147). Neo-liberal logic imposed a single focus on inflation, rather than developing a broader set of macroeconomic management objectives, to the detriment of the Eurozone economy. However, Keynesian monetary policy, operating within the supportive economic infrastructure of an ICU, would be quite different.

Monetary policy within the ICU

The replacement of the current model of EMU with a Keynesian ICU would necessitate a number of fundamental changes. These would include institutional changes, such as the reform of the ECB, the adoption of a new set of policy objectives, replacing price stability with sustaining a system designed to promote balanced trade, full employment and economic growth, and underpinning all of this, a shift in the theoretical foundations about how the economy actually works.

One advantage that the EU has, over those advocating the original Keynes Plan in the 1940s, is that part of the infrastructure necessary for the operation of the scheme is already in place. The ECB already exists as an accepted supranational economic authority, and as such, a reformed Keynesian version of the ECB, perhaps renamed the K-ECB, could form the basis for the clearing agency proposed by Keynes to manage the clearing union. However, the K-ECB would need to operate in a completely different way to the present institution. It would, for example, need to embrace rather different objectives. Rather than the single-minded pursuit of price stability, the K-ECB would take appropriate measures to ensure payments balance and thereby operate the ICU to secure and maintain full employment within the Euro-ICU zone (Davidson, 1992; Arestis, 1999: 9). This would necessitate a radical reform in K-ECB structure, strategic objectives and its willingness to use a broader range of differential policy tools, before it would be an acceptable conduit.

It is an open question as to whether all or most responsibilities to manage the ICU would be devolved to the K-ECB or be divided between different agencies. Combining multiple objectives within a single institution would make co-ordination of strategy more straightforward, but it would have the drawback of making this a particularly powerful organisation. Given the ECB's penchant for engaging in public opinion formation and other areas of political discourse, the vesting of so much authority within one institution might be a cause for concern for many democratically elected officials. Consequently, they may prefer to separate functions concerning the operation of monetary policy and maintenance of the system of exchange-rate pegs, from those relating to financial stability or the design and operation of capital controls or the technical exercise necessary for assessing the need for any adjustments in exchange-rate pegs. Nevertheless, for the purposes of simplicity within this chapter, all functions pertaining to the operation of the ICU are assumed to be devolved to the K-ECB.

If the K-ECB is to be reconstituted as the primary agent of managing the ICU version of EMU, the required shift of objectives and the use of different

policy instruments would require a change in the mind-set of those working for the K-ECB. Recruitment would need to be broadened to become
more accepting of those with Keynesian or less orthodox viewpoints, given
that these central bankers would be required to implement policies designed
to operate within a Keynesian system. The ICU could not function effectively if senior officials within the K-ECB proved to be resistant to the shift
in approach and sought to perpetuate elements of a more orthodox monetary
policy within K-ECB operations. This may prove problematic, given the dominance of orthodox economic perspectives in the finance sector and, albeit to a
lesser extent, in academia – the two areas from which potential K-ECB officials
might be drawn. Nevertheless, given the importance of the new institution for
the success of the new policy orientation, sufficient candidates would need to
be found amongst heterodox economist communities.

The next fundamental reform would be the replacement of the single currency with a Euro-bancor common currency union. This would require the
re-introduction of national currencies, which would all be fixed in relation to
the Euro-bancor. The simplest way of doing this would be to restore previous
national currencies by using the exchange rate pertaining at the moment when
the Euro was created. However, doing so would lock in substantial changes
in economic competitiveness between participating member states, implying
that using this set of exchange rates would no longer reflect economic reality and would not achieve the desired balance of transactions. Consequently,
there might be a pressing need for an immediate realignment of currency pegs
shortly after the ICU had been established, in order to meet the criteria of the
system. Consequently, it might seem more convenient if this realignment were
to be determined in advance of the re-introduction of national currencies, so
that they could start operating as determined by the best available evidence
pertaining at the moment the ICU was created. Essentially, the argument would
be to get any disruption over with immediately upon the switch to the ICU.
However, the timing of when a currency realignment occurred – during or
immediately after the transition to the Euro-bancor – could be left to negotiations between participating nations.

The Euro-bancor would be a form of international bank money, similar
in some ways to the Special Drawing Rights (SDR) or the ECU internal
accounting unit previously used by the EU, in that there would be no physical
manifestations of the currency (i.e. coins, notes) for individuals to hold or use
in transactions. Its purpose, as international bank money, would be used to settle
final international balances between participating member states. Day-to-day
purchases would be undertaken in the restored national currencies. Similarly,
the fact that there would be only one-way convertibility of foreign currencies into Euro-bancor means that there would be no need to provide physical
versions of the currency for the use of trading partners. The K-ECB would
manage this system, ensuring the settlement of balances using Euro-bancor
occurred smoothly.

The reformed K-ECB would ensure that the ICU remained a closed system. Credits would not be permitted to leave the system, as doing so would undermine the creation of a circular flow of income within the Eurozone, and leakages would undermine attempts to sustain a sufficient level of aggregate demand to secure full employment. Hence, foreign exchange transactions must remain within the control of the central banks of each individual participating member state, to be released upon licence for the use of firms or banks as part of international trade, and the K-ECB would need to monitor and enforce this restriction.

For foreign nations trading with the ICU, those running a trade deficit would settle their accounts with the K-ECB as usual, using any previous Euro-bancor credits or utilising other financial securities, whilst those nations running a trade surplus with the ICU could hold credit balances in Euro-bancor rather than their own currencies. The only real difference in this case would be that any excess reserves would be recycled and used within the clearing union in just the same manner as a participating member state with idle balances, and thereby maintaining potential purchasing power in the ICU. Moreover, the foreign nation would have to be content that their balances could only be used within the ICU and not withdrawn from the clearing union.

Capital controls would need to be re-introduced, to prevent unregulated financial flows from undermining the ICU system. The policing of this system would be a key feature of either the K-ECB or a separate supranational economic agency established specifically for the purpose. Payments for international trade would be automatically allowed, whereas shorter term capital movements and speculation would be severely restricted.

Though not strictly monetary policy, the ICU would require either the K-ECB or another form of specially constituted economic agency to monitor the symmetric rebalancing operations of the ICU. In the original Keynes Plan, much of this was intended to occur automatically, as a system of incentives and penalties nudged participating member states running a surplus to use their otherwise idle balances. For example, those nations running a large and persistent trade deficit would be allowed to borrow from the K-ECB directly and/or have the right to devalue their currency to restore their competitive position. Equally, those nations running a large and persistent trade surplus over time, would be expected to take corrective measures, which may include using this surplus to increase aggregate demand in its own economy, use it to facilitate FDI or loans to deficit nations to increase their output capacity, or to appreciate their currency. If sizeable balances remained, the K-ECB would impose a *negative* rate of interest upon these credit balances, such that nations with idle balances would have to pay the central bank for the privilege of leaving this money in their account. Moreover, the K-ECB or a separately constituted ICU investment fund, would have the right to lend some or all of this amount to deficit nations.

The recycling of reserves facilitates the maintenance of a higher level of effective demand within the ICU (Davidson, 1992: 8; Arestis, 1999: 9). It would replicate some of the functions of the existing Trans-European Automated Real-Time Gross Settlement Express Transfer System (TARGET2) clearing and settlement system that has been operating in the Eurozone (Lavoie, 2015: 7). However, since the current variant of EMU precludes adjustments in exchange rates, any large scale adjustments would be considerably more painful for the economies concerned than under the Keynesian ICU alternative (Cesaratto, 2013: 369–370). Furthermore, the pressure exerted by the ICU to recycle idle balances contrasts sharply with the practice within the current Eurozone, where credits are rewarded by a *positive* interest rate equal to the ECB target rate (Lavoie, 2015: 15).

The stabilisation of ICU economies additionally necessitates the maintenance of financial stability across the ICU zone. This need not be imposed by the K-ECB, albeit that EMU would infer a degree of co-ordination across whatever agencies were selected for this task. This could be the national central banks, or a Central Financial Agency (CFA) as suggested by Arestis and Sawyer (2013b: 10–11). Whatever the form, the stabilisation of financial markets would require the financial stability agency seeking to influence the credit and lending policies of the full range of financial institutions. It would involve both macroprudential and microprudential measures.

Macroprudential policy may include seeking to control the size, leverage, fragility and risk of the financial system. One example of this approach might be to re-introduce quantitative controls, such as varying capital adequacy ratios, loan-to-value ratios and tighter repayment periods, depending upon risk assessment not only for the institutions themselves but additionally for the stability of the financial sector and economy as a whole (D'Arista, 2009: 12). Moreover, macroprudential measures would likely operate in a countercyclical manner and seek to prevent the growth of asset price bubbles (Arestis and Karakitsos, 2009). This is a tricky exercise, because central banks additionally need to act as lender of last resort and supply liquidity to the banking system whenever required (Arestis and Sawyer, 2010: 109; De Grauwe, 2013). Thus, there might be a need to combine financial stabilisation approaches with aspects of fiscal policy, since asset prices are impacted by inequitable ownership of these assets, and therefore an element of redistribution may assist macroprudential goals.

Microprudential policy would complement macroprudential measures. It might, for example, seek to reduce the size of banks that are currently 'too big to fail' and re-introduce the sort of division between retail and investment banking as previously contained in 'Glass-Steagall' legislation in the USA (Arestis and Karakitsos, 2013). It may also seek to discourage those types of investments that might prove particularly risky to the economy as a whole – certain types of derivatives would certainly fall into this category – by, for example, restricting deposit guarantees to the more conservative institutions (Arestis and Sawyer, 2013a: 154–155).

One criticism of the ICU proposal concerns the potential inflationary effects that may arise out of its operations. For example, Meltzer (1983: 19) claims that Keynes was aware of the possible inflationary bias of his scheme, due to an excess supply of money, but that this flaw was not addressed. He suggests that this may have been because the scheme was unlikely to be accepted by the American negotiators at the Bretton Woods summit. The argument is advanced that the ICU provides surplus nations with an incentive to expand their economy, rather than allow build-up of surpluses triggering an exchange-rate appreciation. Similarly, persistent deficit nations would be expected to devalue, which would improve the competitiveness of their exports but also provide an expansionary effect. In combination, these two measures would provide a stimulus to economic activity across the ICU. If economies were already operating at full employment levels, then this would be inflationary.

This critique ignores the basic starting point which led to the development of the Keynes Plan in the first place, namely that the operation of the current international payments system – through asymmetric treatment of deficit and surplus nations, alongside the amassing of idle reserves – has a profound *deflationary* effect upon the global economy (Keynes, 1980: 46–48, 60, 74–77, 112–113). The ICU was *supposed* to reverse this effect, thereby providing better global balance. Moreover, it would do so with no burden placed upon surplus nations (Keynes, 1980: 112, 115). If this analysis is correct, then it is likely that the global economy would 'run hotter', with less wasted resources, and the varied evidence arising from Phillips Curve, NAIRU and other policy trade-off analysis, would indicate that inflationary pressures may arise at slightly less than full employment equilibrium. Nevertheless, even if this analysis is correct, this is more of a problem for the correct use of macroeconomic policy tools, rather than a justification to reject the ICU system.

Conclusion

Monetary policy would be subservient to the requirements of managing the common currency area in the Keynesian ICU model of EMU. The focus would shift from price stability to broader objectives of creating the conditions which would best facilitate the sustainable achievement of full employment and economic growth in participating economies. Released from the constraints imposed by the adoption of a single currency and a monetary policy approach dominated by flawed theoretical assumptions of a self-managing economy always and rapidly returning to full employment equilibrium, the ICU approach would provide a supportive infrastructure that would encourage systematic rebalancing of the Eurozone economies without pushing deficit nations into a spiral of austerity, slow growth and unemployment. The reformed K-ECB would retain its leadership role within the alternative form of EMU, but its new focus would be on the stability of the system as a whole and acting to prevent the growth of financial instability.

Bibliography

Akerlof, G.A., Dickens, W.T. and Perry, G.L. (1996), 'The Macroeconomics of Low Inflation', *Brookings Papers on Economic Activity*, 27(1): 1–76.

Alesina, A. (1988), 'Macroeconomics and Politics', in *NBER Macroeconomic Annual*, MIT Press, Cambridge, MA.

Alesina, A. (1989), 'Politics and Business Cycles in Industrial Democracies', *Economic Policy*, 8: 58–98.

Alesina, A. and Grilli, V. (1991), 'The European Central Bank: Reshaping Monetary Policies in Europe', *CEPR Discussion Paper* No. 563. Available via: www.nber.org/papers/w3860.pdf.

Alesina, A. and Summers, L. (1993), 'Central Bank Independence and Macroeconomic Performance: Some Comparative Evidence', *Journal of Money, Credit and Banking*, 25(2): 1–14.

Arestis, P. (1989), 'On the Post-Keynesian Challenge to Neo-Classical Economics: A Complete Quantitative Macro-Model for the UK Economy', *Journal of Post-Keynesian Economics*, 11(4): 611–629.

Arestis, P. (1999), 'The Independent European Central Bank: Keynesian Alternatives', *Jerome Levy Economics Institute Working Paper* No. 274. Available via: https://papers.ssrn.com/sol3/papers.cfm?abstract_id=174852.

Arestis, P. and Karakitsos, E. (2009), 'Unemployment and the Natural Interest Rate in a Neo-Wicksellian Model', in Arestis, P. and McCombie, J. (Eds.), *Unemployment: Past and Present*, Houndmills, Palgrave, Basingstoke.

Arestis, P. and Karakitsos, E. (2013), *Financial Stability in the Aftermath of the 'Great Recession'*, Palgrave, Basingstoke.

Arestis, P., McCauley, K. and Sawyer, M. (2001), 'An Alternative Stability Pact for the European Union', *Cambridge Journal of Economics*, 25(1): 113–130.

Arestis, P. and Sawyer, M. (2004), *Re-Examining Monetary and Fiscal Policy for the 21st Century*, Edward Elgar, Cheltenham.

Arestis, P. and Sawyer, M. (2010), '21st Century Keynesian Economic Policies', in Arestis, P. and Sawyer, M. (Eds.), *21st Century Keynesian Economics*, Palgrave, Basingstoke, 81–120.

Arestis, P. and Sawyer, M. (2013a), *Economic and Monetary Union Macroeconomic Policies*, Palgrave, Basingstoke.

Arestis, P. and Sawyer, M. (2013b), 'The "New Economics" and Policies for Financial Stability', in Arestis, P. and Sawyer, M. (Eds.), *Economic Policies of the New Thinking in Economics*, Routledge, London, 3–16.

Ball, L. and Sheridan, N. (2003), 'Does Inflation Targeting Matter?', *NBER Working Paper* No. 9577, National Bureau of Economic Research, Cambridge, MA. Available via: www.nber.org/chapters/c9561.pdf.

Barro, R. and Gordon, D. (1983), 'Rules, Discretion, and Reputation in a Model of Monetary Policy', *Journal of Monetary Economics*, 12(1): 101–121.

Bell, D.E., Raiffa, H. and Tversky, A. (1988), *Decision Making: Descriptive, Normative and Prescriptive Interactions*, Cambridge University Press, Cambridge.

Bernanke, B.S., Laubach, T., Mishkin, F.S. and Posen, A. (1999), *Inflation Targeting: Lessons From International Experience*, Princeton University Press, Princeton, NJ.

Bibow, J. (2004), 'Reflections on the Current Fashion for Central Bank Independence', *Cambridge Journal of Economics*, 28(4): 549–576.

Bibow, J. (2009), *Keynes in Monetary Policy, Finance and Uncertainty*, Routledge, Abingdon.

Bibow, J. (2010), 'Bretton Woods 2 Is Dead, Long Live Bretton Woods 3?', *Levy Economics Institute Working Paper* No. 597. Available via: www.levyinstitute.org/pubs/wp_597.pdf.

Blanchard, O. and Summers, L. (1988), 'Beyond the Natural Rate Hypothesis', *American Economic Review*, 78(2): 182–187.

Blinder, A.S. (1998), *Central Banking in Theory and Practice*, MIT Press, Cambridge, MA.

Caporaso, J.A. and Levine, D.P. (1992), *Theories of Political Economy*, Cambridge University Press, Cambridge.

Carvalho, F. (1995), 'The Independence of Central Banks: A Critical Assessment of the Arguments', *Journal of Post Keynesian Economics*, 18(2): 159–176.

Cesaratto, S. (2013), 'The Implications of TARGET2 in the European Balance of Payments Crisis and Beyond', *European Journal of Economics and Economic Policies: Intervention*, 10(3): 359–382.

Clift, B. (2001), 'New Labour's Third Way and European Social Democracy', in Ludlam, S. and Smith, M.J. (Eds.), *New Labour in Government*, Macmillan, London, 55–73.

Cornwall, J. and Cornwall, W. (1998), 'Unemployment Costs and Inflation Targeting', in Arestis, P. and Sawyer, M. (Eds.), *The Political Economy of Central Banking*, Edward Elgar, Cheltenham, 49–66.

Cukierman, A. (1992), *Central Bank Strategy, Credibility and Independence*, MIT Press, Cambridge, MA.

Cukierman, A. (1994), 'Central Bank Independence and Monetary Control', *Economic Journal*, 104(427): 1437–1448.

D'Arista, J. (2009), 'Setting an Agenda for Monetary Reform', *Political Economy Research Institute Working Paper* No. 190. Available via: http://scholarworks.umass.edu/cgi/viewcontent.cgi?article=1159&context=peri_workingpapers.

Davidson, P. (1992), 'Reforming the World's Money', *Journal of Post Keynesian Economics*, 15(2): 153–179.

Davidson, P. (1995), 'Uncertainty in Economics', in Dow, S. and Hilliard, J. (Eds.), *Keynes, Knowledge and Uncertainty*, Edward Elgar, Cheltenham, 107–116.

Debelle, G. and Fischer, G. (1994), 'How Independent Should a Central Bank Be?', in Fuhrer, J.C. (Ed.), *Goals, Guidelines and Constraints Facing Monetary Policymaker*, Federal Reserve Bank of Boston, Boston, MA, 195–221.

De Grauwe, P. (2013), 'Design Failures in the Eurozone: Can They Be Fixed?', *European Economy Economics Papers*, No. 491, European Commission, Brussels. Available via: http://ec.europa.eu/economy_finance/publications/economic_paper/2013/pdf/ecp491_en.pdf.

ECB (2011), *The Monetary Policy of the ECB*, ECB, Frankfurt.

EU Commission (1992), *Treaty on European Union*, Office for the Official Publications of the European Communities, Luxembourg.

Fischer, A.M. (1996), 'Central Bank Independence and Sacrifice Ratios', *Open Economies Review*, 7(1): 5–18.

Friedman, M. (1960), *A Programme for Monetary Stability*, Fordham University Press, New York.

Friedman, M. (1968), 'The Role of Monetary Policy', *American Economic Review*, 58(1): 1–17.

Friedman, M. (1972), 'The Case for a Monetary Rule', *Newsweek*, 7 February.

Galbraith, J.K. (1997), 'Time to Ditch the NAIRU', *Journal of Economic Perspectives*, 11(1): 93–108.

Grilli, V., Masciandaro, D. and Tabellini, G. (1991), 'Political and Monetary Institutions and Public Financial Policies in the Industrialised Countries', *Economic Policy*, 6(13): 341–392.

Hillman, A.L. (1999), 'Political Culture and the Political Economy of Central Bank Independence', in Blejer, M. and Streb, M. (Eds.), *Major Issues in Central Banking, Monetary Policy and Implications for Transition Economies*, Kluwer, Amsterdam.

IMF (1996), *World Economic Outlook*, IMF, New York.

Issing, O. (2002), *Should We Have Faith in Central Banks?* Institute of Economic Affairs, London.

Issing, O., Gaspar, V., Angeloni, I. and Tristani, O. (2001), *Monetary Policy in the Euro Area: Strategy and Decision Making at the European Central Bank*, Cambridge University Press, Cambridge.

Jabko, N. (1999), 'In the Name of the Market: How the European Commission Paved the Way for Monetary Union', *Journal of European Public Policy*, 6(3): 475–495.

Jordan, T.J. (1997), 'Disinflation Costs, Accelerating Inflation Gains and Central Bank Independence', *Weltwirtschaftliches Archiv*, 133(1): 1–21.

Jordan, T.J. (1999), 'Central Bank Independence and the Sacrifice Ratio', *European Journal of Political Economy*, 15(2): 229–255.

Kahneman, D., Slovic, P. and Tversky, A. (1982), *Judgement Under Uncertainty*, Cambridge University Press, Cambridge.

Kalecki, M. (1971), *Selected Essays on the Dynamics of the Capitalist Economy 1933–1970*, Cambridge University Press, Cambridge.

Keynes, J.M. (1930), *A Treatise on Money, Vol. 2: The Applied Theory of Money*, Macmillan, London.

Keynes, J.M. (1933), *The Means to Prosperity*, Macmillan, London.

Keynes, J.M. (1936), *The General Theory of Employment, Interest and Money*, Macmillan, London, 1973 edition.

Keynes, J.M. (1979), 'The General Theory and After: A Supplement', In Moggridge, D. (Ed.), *The Collected Writings of John Maynard Keynes*, Vol. 24, Macmillan, London.

Keynes, J.M. (1980), *The Collected Writings of J.M. Keynes: Vol. 25 – Activities 1940–44: Shaping the Postwar World – The Clearing Union*, D. Moggridge (Ed.), Cambridge University Press, Cambridge.

Kyland, F. and Prescott, E. (1977), 'Rules Rather Than Discretion: The Inconsistency of Optimal Plans', *Journal of Political Economy*, 85(3): 473–492.

Lavoie, M. (2015), 'The Eurozone: Similarities to and Differences From Keynes's Plan', *International Journal of Political Economy*, 44(1): 3–17.

Lawson, T. (1995), 'Economics and Expectations', in Dow, S. and Hilliard, J. (Eds.), *Keynes, Knowledge and Uncertainty*, Edward Elgar, Cheltenham, 77–106.

Lucas, R. (1976), 'Econometric Policy Evaluation: A Critique', in Brunner, K. and Meltzer, A. (Eds.), *Carnegie-Rochester Series in Public Policy*, 1, North-Holland, Amsterdam, 19–46.

Meltzer, A.H. (1983), 'Keynes on Monetary Reform and International Economic Order', Paper presented at the *5th Henry Thornton Lecture*, 3 October, City University Business School, London. Available via: http://repository.cmu.edu/tepper/796/.

Micosso, S. (2015), 'The Monetary Policy of the European Central Bank (2002–2015)', *CEPS Special Report* No. 109. Available via: www.ceps.eu/system/files/SR%20109%20 SM%20Monetary%20Policy%20of%20the%20ECB_0.pdf.

Nordhaus, W. (1975), 'The Political Business Cycle', *Review of Economic Studies*, 42(2): 169–190.

Phelps, E.S. (1968), 'Money-Wage Dynamics and Labor Market Equilibrium', *Journal of Political Economy*, 76(4S): 678–711.

Posen, A.S. (1995), 'Central Bank Independence and Dis-Inflationary Credibility: A Missing Link?', *Staff Report* 1, Federal Reserve Bank of New York, New York.

Recio, A. and Roca, J. (1998), 'The Spanish Socialists in Power: Thirteen Years of Economic Policy', *Oxford Review of Economic Policy*, 14(1): 139–158.

Rogoff, K. (1985), 'The Optimum Degree of Commitment to an Intermediate Monetary Target', *Quarterly Journal of Economics*, 100(4): 1169–1189.

Rowthorn, R.E. (1995), 'Capital Formation and Unemployment', *Oxford Review of Economic Policy*, 11(1): 26–39.

Sepehri, A. and Moshiri, S. (2004), 'Inflation-Growth Profiles Across Countries: Evidence From Developing and Developed Countries', *International Review of Applied Economics*, 18(2): 191–208.

Shafir, E. (Ed.) (2004), *Performance, Belief and Similarity: Selected Writings of Amos Tversky*, MIT Press, Cambridge, MA.

Stiglitz, J. (2002), *Globalization and Its Discontents*, Penguin, London.

Stiglitz, J. (2003), *The Roaring Nineties: Seeds of Destruction*, Penguin, London.

Stiglitz, J.A. (2016), *The Euro and Its Threat to the Future of Europe*, Allen Lane, London.

Taylor, J.B. (1993), 'Discretion versus Policy Rules in Practice', *Carnegie-Rochester Conference Series on Public Policy*, 39(1): 195–214.

4 Rediscovering fiscal policy

[T]his *long run* is a misleading guide to current affairs. *In the long run* we are all dead. Economists set themselves too easy, too useless a task if in tempestuous seasons they can only tell us that when the storm is long past the ocean will be flat again.

(Keynes, 1923: 80)

Introduction

Participation in EMU involves national governments relinquishing exchange-rate and monetary policy instruments to federal economic authorities. The significance of this loss of policy tools available to manage individual economies depends upon the extent to which devaluation retains a real effect in the medium to long term and whether the financial markets within Europe are so closely integrated that independent monetary policy has been rendered impotent. In addition, the stability of EMU depends upon whether external shocks exert an asymmetric impact upon individual participating countries (Weber, 1991; Bayoumi and Eichengreen, 1993). This is where events occurring outside the Eurozone, whether related to shifts in the demand for certain goods and services in specific industries or asset price bubbles, or alternatively supply-side events such as increases in raw materials and oil prices, may impact disproportionately upon certain countries within the EMU than others. If so, then the external shock has asymmetric effects on different members of the EMU and this is a more difficult task for those seeking to manage the Eurozone economy than if an external shock impacted similarly upon all participants, in which case a common policy change would be suitable for all participants.

Economic theory suggests that the more open an economy, the more it promotes diversity and hence should be less impacted by sector-specific external shocks (McKinnon, 1963). Thus, asymmetric shocks may be minimised if monetary union occurs between countries with comparable industrial structures which are, simultaneously, highly diversified. The expectation is that diversification will cause industry-specific shocks to offset one another, thereby reducing the asymmetric macroeconomic effect, whilst simultaneously assisting supranational policymakers to deal with the consequences of relatively symmetrical shocks (EC Commission, 1990; Emerson et al., 1992). However, this is a contentious idea, as other theorists have argued that the prevalence of regional asymmetric shocks, within existing EU nation states, may equally indicate that the industrial concentration accompanying economic integration may magnify the frequency and importance of asymmetric shocks (De Grauwe and Vanhaverbeke, 1993: 112–125).

To the extent that asymmetric shocks do occur, the Optimum Currency Area (OCA) theory suggests that a combination of factor mobility (Mundell, 1961) and/or fiscal integration (Kenen, 1969) may assist in stabilising the EMU zone (Baimbridge and Whyman, 2008: 87–92). Factor mobility may refer to either labour or capital flexibility. However, labour mobility within European countries has been estimated to be three times lower than in the USA, despite the existence of greater regional inequality and unemployment in Europe, implying that EU labour mobility is less responsive to employment and income incentives than the US labour market (OECD, 1986; Eichengreen, 1992; Goodhart and Smith, 1993: 422). Capital mobility can, in principal, substitute for labour mobility in the long run, as the relocation of productive processes to depressed, inexpensive areas may occur. And, indeed, the early years of the single currency were characterised by a significant movement of capital from the core EU economies, such as Germany and the Netherlands, to its peripheral nations, especially Spain and Greece. However, rather than prompting the seamless facilitation of economic catch-up and promotion of stabilisation that advocates were predicting, this example of a self-generated asymmetric shock resulted in higher wage and inflation rates in peripheral nations. When the capital transfer came to an abrupt halt, and indeed, patterns of FDI reverted to their traditional flows towards core EU economies, this left peripheral economies in an uncompetitive position and having to resort to very painful and slow (internal devaluation) adjustment (Krugman, 2012: 444). In addition, due to the transactions costs involved, factor movements are an inefficient means of reacting to transitory regional shocks (von Hagen, 1993: 278).

The persistence of asymmetric shocks, together with the unrealistic assumptions of those relying upon the perfect function of market determination to secure a full employment equilibrium, and the fact that EMU in Europe was created with inadequately converged economies, have all made the stabilisation of the Eurozone more difficult to achieve (Bayoumi and Eichengreen, 1993). Consequently, there would appear to be an a priori case for supporting the use of fiscal policy as the primary stabilising instrument and an, albeit imperfect, substitute for exchange-rate flexibility (Kenen, 1969, 1995: 81; Masson, 1996: 1002). However, this has proven to be controversial amongst European policymakers, with the ECB, in particular, resistant to a greater role for active fiscal policy as a stabilisation measure. Indeed, as we shall discuss in this chapter, the current momentum across the Eurozone is for a tighter, more constrained approach to fiscal policy and a greater reliance upon market determination. This chapter, then, will assess whether this is the correct fiscal policy stance to adopt and whether there are superior alternatives to consider.

Current EMU model – restraining fiscal policy

In the current conception of EMU, fiscal policy is viewed as having a relatively weak impact upon the real economy. It should therefore be constrained to prevent inflationary pressures and also debt being incurred which may undermine the financial viability of the currency union. Fiscal rules were adopted intending to prevent free rider problems arising via the ability of individual member states being able to borrow in a common currency and potential moral hazard if political pressure necessitates the bailing out of any nation borrowing excessively (Lane, 2012: 49). It has been suggested that fiscal "discipline" is "fundamental" for macroeconomic stability and hence laying the foundations for future economic growth (ECB, 2005: 7). Thus, the fiscal architecture of EMU is designed to explicitly constrain the autonomy and flexibility of national fiscal policy amongst EMU participants. In particular, it is intended to prevent member states from running large budget deficits and public sector debts, which have been determined as incompatible with the long-term stability of the system (EC Commission, 1990).

The fiscal rules formed two parts, both focused upon emphasising the self-discipline of participating member states (Degryse, 2012: 12). The first, pre-participation, involved the Maastricht convergence criteria (MCC), which set out five financial tests which potential members were supposed to meet prior to acceptance as full members of EMU. These rules were criticised as being too narrowly focused on financial rather than real economy effects, nevertheless, whether or not the convergence criteria were insufficiently developed, the failure to adequately police their implementation has cast its shadow over the contemporary problems with public debt in Greece, Cyprus, Italy and Spain. Post-participation, the Stability and Growth Pact (SGP), derived from the 1997 Amsterdam Treaty, sought to make permanent and transparent the public finance obligations contained in the MCC. Articles 121 and 126 of the Treaty on the Functioning of the European Union (TFEU) provide the legal basis of the SGP and establishing the proscribed limits of 3 per cent of GDP for budget deficits and 60 per cent of GDP for public debt.[1]

The theoretical basis for the SGP derives from what has been variously termed the 'new monetarism' (Arestis and Sawyer, 1998) or the 'new consensus' approach, which effectively synthesises concepts drawn from monetarism and New Keynesian economic schools of thought (Arestis, 2007). This holds that:

1   Inflation is a monetary phenomenon (Friedman, 1956) and can be controlled through monetary policy, which is either aimed at controlling the money supply directly or via indirect influence through inflation targeting, as the central bank setting the key ('repo') interest rate.
2   The economy fluctuates around the economic concept of the non-accelerating inflation rate of unemployment (NAIRU), whereby supply-side factors determine real economic variables such as unemployment and output (Layard and Nickell, 1985; Carlin and Soskice, 1990).

3   Following on from (2.), the resulting policy stance is to maintain a neutral fiscal policy and reply primarily upon monetary policy, through the medium of the interest rate policy instrument, to smooth demand shocks and thereby enable supply-side factors to determine development in the real economy.

4   Consequently, there is no need for democratic control over fiscal or monetary policy, as these are supportive to the primary drivers of economic growth, and therefore these instruments can be subcontracted to technocratic specialists in the ECB and/or be constrained by the operation of the SGP. Indeed, democratic intervention in the process is viewed as harmful, since 'irresponsible' politicians are assumed to pursue short-term popularity at the cost of generating longer term inflationary pressures. Arguments pertaining to time-inconsistent behaviour and the inflation bias syndrome (Kydland and Prescott, 1977; Barro and Gordon, 1983) were discussed in the previous chapter.

Critique of the SGP

The design and operation of the SGP has, however, been criticised in two rather different ways. The first critique argues that the design of the SGP is viewed as fundamentally flawed in a number of respects. For example, the rigidity of the SGP does not allow for the possibility of fiscal policy being operated differently, in each individual member state, to better accord with the preferences of individual electoral preferences (Copelovitch et al., 2016). In addition, the SGP is asymmetric in reinforcing national budgetary behaviour to the benefit of the monetary union as a whole (Monperrus-Veroni and Saraceno, 2006: 33–34). Moreover, the theoretical foundations of NAIRU are certainly not without quite substantive criticism (Setterfield et al., 1992; Galbraith, 1997; Whyman, 2006: 65–68).

The most significant problem, however, concerns its frustration of successful national macroeconomic management, by denying national governments the flexibility required to operate countercyclical demand management policies (Burkitt et al., 1996; Arestis and Sawyer, 2013; Baimbridge and Whyman, 2015). Governments should be aiming to promote economic stability and economic growth through the maintenance of a sufficient level of effective demand in the economy, together with interventions aimed at enhancing the performance of labour markets and industrial competitiveness. This may require a greater flexibility in public finances than allowed under the SGP. Therefore, the latter may prevent corrective measures necessary to prevent recessionary conditions, with the resultant loss of economic potential and human cost. It has been calculated that, if its provisions had been applied to recessionary episodes during previous time periods, the SGP would have constrained not only those member states which entered the period of economic slowdown with an existing budget deficit, but also negatively affected a number of nations who were running a budget surplus (Buti et al., 1997: 29).

Another substantive critique of the SGP claims that, rather than it being a flawed concept, it is incomplete and thereby insufficiently robust to secure the financial rectitude necessitated of all participants in a monetary union. This belief was reinforced by the ability of large member states, including France and Germany, to periodically ignore the proscriptive nature of the SGP when they have not found the rules convenient, and when they have been faced with determined domestic opposition by organised labour (Bieler, 2006: 210; Mathers, 2007: 3). Consequently, reforms were advocated which would strengthen existing rules intended to prevent the emergence of large fiscal deficits and public debt within individual member states, to prevent the Eurozone being undermined by individual nations either requiring bailing out by other members, or defaulting and placing the future of the single currency at risk.

The flaws inherent within the MCC and SGP would be less significant had perfect convergence occurred before member states were permitted to participate in the single currency. However, the short-term political gain in facilitating maximum participation in the single currency has exacerbated medium-term problems in the Eurozone. The persistence of asymmetric external shocks requires an alternative stabilising mechanism to be developed to prevent monetary union being undermined by diverse economic and social forces. Previous examples of fixed currency regimes, which were not based upon firm national identity, have collapsed in similar circumstances. Examples include the Scandinavian Currency Union, the Latin Monetary Union, the Gold Standard, the Modified Gold Standard and Bretton Woods.

Unfortunately, the significance of this lesson appears to have been overlooked by the EU, when devising its response to the 2008 financial crisis. Instead of the SGP being replaced by a more flexible set of budgetary rules, intended to ensure a sufficient level of aggregate demand exists in each member state to facilitate full employment, the EUs response was to further tighten fiscal scrutiny and place narrower limits upon fiscal manoeuvrability.

Response to crisis – the fiscal compact

The 2008 international financial crisis, which was triggered by problems related to sub-prime housing loans and securitisation via collateralised loan obligations and credit default swops, led to a deep economic recession across most of the industrialised world. It highlighted not only the fragility of the European banking system, but additionally the flaws in design of the particular form of Economic and Monetary Union (EMU) established amongst a number of European Union (EU) member states. The tensions caused by the financial crisis have not caused these problems, however, but rather magnified pre-existing weaknesses which have long been recognised by a selection of the academic commentators who have written on this topic over the past two decades or more (Eichengreen, 1992; De Grauwe and Vanhaverbeke, 1993; Burkitt et al., 1996; Feldstein, 1997; Arestis and Sawyer, 2000; Lane, 2006). Moreover, it is not only the design of EMU, and the rules established to limit participation to suitable candidate nations which have been found to be at fault, but also the economic architecture introduced in an attempt to sustain this new arrangement (Degryse, 2012: 6).

The response to these problems has been to combine limited financial assistance with tighter controls upon the ability of national governments to manage their own economies. In terms of the former, the EU member states have sought to provide emergency loans to assist EMU members in immediate and pressing difficulties, in order to prevent nations being forced to leave the single currency or, indeed, for EMU to disintegrate. This has been called the 'kicking the can down the road' approach, as it is a temporary 'sticking plaster' and does not solve fundamental problems, but might create the time for this to occur. Financial assistance has evolved into a more substantive European Stability Mechanism, but where financial loans are provided, they are subject to the implementation of austerity measures and reforms in national labour and/or social policy, intended to reduce public expenditure (Bird and Mandilaras, 2012: 4).

The 'fiscal compact' is the second element of the response and it embodies the latest example of the trend towards imposing tighter restrictions upon the ability of national governments to operate fiscal policy within Europe (Bird and Mandilaras, 2012: 3). The compact is established by the Treaty on Stability, Coordination and Governance in the Economic and Monetary Union (TSCG) and it includes (Bird and Mandilaras, 2012: 4):

- Member states are required to introduce a balanced-budget rule, by legislation or constitutional amendment, which necessitates general government budgets to be either balanced or in surplus, with an annual structural deficit not exceeding 0.5 per cent of GDP. It would appear that the severity of this constraint is to be more flexibly interpreted for those member states with public debt below 60 per cent of GDP. Nevertheless, the failure to adopt a balanced-budget rule will trigger the Commission fining the member state in question up to 0.1 per cent of its GDP.
- Member states are required to introduce an automatic mechanism, via legislation, designed to correct any fiscal deficits deemed to be 'excessive' by this balanced-budget rule. Member states are additionally required to submit, to both the Commission and Council, a programme of fiscal measures designed to ensure that the balance budget rule is met.
- Those member states with public debt exceeding 60 per cent GDP are required to reduce it by an average rate of 5 per cent per year.
- The Commission and the Council are empowered to monitor the progress made by the member state(s) in achieving these goals and they can reject proposals for fiscal retrenchment that they do not believe will adequately address perceived deficits and/or levels of accumulated public debt. This external surveillance and imposition of mandatory penalties for breaches of the fiscal compact rules are unprecedented for the EU; they severely limit the scope for subsidiarity in the national determination of fiscal policy.

The design of the fiscal compact is not, however, without criticism. For example, as was discussed in Chapter 2 of this book, the EU response to the financial crisis has been to mistake *effect* for the *cause* of the problems in the Eurozone, by focusing upon perceived problems with 'excessive' fiscal deficits and debt, rather than focusing upon the more significant structural and trade imbalances within the single currency zone. Interestingly, Stiglitz (2016: 202) notes that, at the time the crisis occurred, even Greek debt (at around 109 per cent of GDP), was lower than US and UK debt at the end of the Second World War (118 per cent and 250 per cent of GDP respectively), and below Japan's current debt (246 per cent of GDP). Indeed, during this period of relatively high levels of national debt, the USA recorded a period of particularly rapid economic growth (Stiglitz, 2016: 211), thereby suggesting that in its response to the financial crisis, the USA chose to stimulate its economy, thereby incurring higher (temporary) public debt, and grew more rapidly than other comparable economies. Thus, the link between debt leading to lower growth does not appear to be quite as straightforward as those designing the Eurozone's response to the financial crisis might wish to believe.

Advocates of the fiscal compact approach would appear to judge that fiscal deficits lead to current account deficits, and are therefore unsustainable. However, it is entirely plausible, using basic national accounting rules, to demonstrate that budget deficits may arise due to excessive savings in the private sector, whilst current account deficits may arise alongside budget surpluses (Bird and Mandilaras, 2012: 7–8). Thus, the fiscal compact response is, at best, a simplistic reaction to a generalisation of the causes of fiscal deficits. Fiscal deficits need to be evaluated in the context of the overall macroeconomic picture; whether they are excessive depends upon a range of other factors, including the size of the output gap, private-sector imbalances, the level of public debt, the relationship between fiscal deficits and economic growth which may vary over the economic cycle (Bird and Mandilaras, 2012: 17). Thus, whilst the fiscal compact may aim at reducing the incidence of economic crises, it does little to achieve this goal and, moreover, it reduces the effectiveness of policy instruments which in turn increases the difficulty in dealing with future crises. Consequently, a policy designed to strengthen the Eurozone may have precisely the opposite effect (Bird and Mandilaras, 2012: 22).

Theoretical underpinning to constraining fiscal policy

The rationale for the fiscal compact further restricting the capability of fiscal policy, is drawn from a set of neo-liberal propositions. At its most basic, New Classical economics proposes that markets clear instantly and, as a result, adjustment to the supply-side equilibrium occurs immediately, leaving no room for an active fiscal policy. The New Keynesian–New Monetarist consensus, that dominates contemporary economics, accedes that fiscal policy may have an impact in the short run, but it accepts the New Classical argument in the long run. These schools of economics, in turn, have developed a number of inter-connected arguments that question the effectiveness of fiscal policy.

The first of these propositions is derived from monetarist arguments that instead of raising aggregate demand, rising government spending would be off-set by falling private investment due to a crowding-out effect (Meerpol, 1998: 42). This could occur if a fiscal expansion caused an increase in interest rates, which in turn deterred private investment (Neville, 2000: 159). This could, however, only occur if the economy conformed to the neo-classical concep-tion of a money market, where there is a finite supply of money available at each equilibrium interest rate, rather than accepting the premise that money is, in large part, created by the banking sector. Or else, alternatively, if adopting the post-Keynesian assumption of endogenous money, then monetary authori-ties would have to raise interest rates to presumably prevent the generation of inflationary pressures and therefore deliberately offset the intent informing the original fiscal expansion.

A second variant of the crowding-out theory claims that rising fiscal expenditure will result in a larger budget deficit (or smaller surplus) and therefore the government will consume an increasing proportion of private savings and therefore crowd out private investment (Friedman, 1962: 81). This is an old argument that dates back to the 1930s British 'Treasury view' which opposed public works schemes on the basis that spending on these initia-tives would displace an equal amount of private-sector investment spending, despite ample evidence of resources laying idle due to mass unemployment and underutilisation of productive capacity (Palley, 1998: 141). Once again, this argument is based upon the assumption of exogenous money and a resultant given level of savings, whereas post-Keynesian theory holds that an expansion of effective demand will stimulate investment which, in turn, will generate additional income and thereby boost rather than reduce savings. It additionally ignores the potential for a balanced-budget multiplier, where an increase in both government expenditure and revenue provides a stimulus to the economy due to the fact that the marginal propensity to spend public expenditure is higher than the private consumption lost due to the com-mensurate rise in taxation (Neville, 2000: 159). Although, in most cases, the limited stimulus provided by this mechanism would be insufficient in the fact of recessionary pressures, and therefore the criticism of deficit financing reappears.

A final variant suggests that crowding out will occur because the economy tends, in the long run, towards a NAIRU or natural rate of unemployment supply-side determined equilibrium and, as a result, fiscal policy expansion will be ineffective. The problem here is that, in the absence of market forces sufficiently powerful to ensure a rapid adjustment in aggregate demand to be consistent with the supply-side equilibrium, fiscal policy can certainly have an effect. Not surprisingly, given the importance of this point for the signifi-cance attached to active macroeconomic policy, different schools of economic thought fundamentally disagree with one another.

The second set of arguments suggest that time lags inherent within the budgetary and fiscal policy implementation programmes lead to the mistiming of fiscal boosts and reductions, thereby exacerbating business cycles rather than counteracting their fluctuations (Hemming, Kell et al., 2002). Since governments only typically have one or possibly two budgets per year, and these are subject to parliamentary scrutiny and debate, it is likely that these events will not correspond exactly to the needs of the economy (Alesina et al., 2006: 1–2). Once approved, there will be a further implementation time lag, until fiscal measures impact upon aggregate demand and thereby the real economy. As a result, it is suggested that these time lags may cause fiscal policy to be sufficiently delayed as to become pro-cyclical rather than countercyclical (Friedman, 1962: 38).

Of course, there are ways to reduce time lags through forward planning of potential intervention scenarios, such as the Swedish investment funds to take but one example (Whyman, 2006: 81). Moreover, these arguments lose some of their validity when interventions are timely, well designed and focused (Elmendorf and Furman, 2008). In addition, since automatic stabilisers are typically insufficient by themselves as a stabilising mechanism, unless the remaining instability is ignored through employing the assumption of an economy continuously at or close to full employment, then there is a strong justification for augmenting automatic stabilisers with discretionary fiscal policy (Arestis and Sawyer, 2013: 160).

A third set of arguments are based upon the New Classical notion of Ricardian equivalence, in that increasing fiscal deficits might cause households to defer their immediate consumption in anticipation of higher government spending foreshadowing higher levels of future taxation. As a result, the fiscal boost is offset by consumer behaviour and is ineffective (Cwik and Wieland, 2010). However, Ricardian equivalence is not particularly well supported by the evidence (Hemming, Kell et al., 2002: 36). Indeed, this proposition rests upon assumptions of full employment, where ex ante savings are equal to ex ante investment, and there is a presumption that Say's Law operates. Consequently, the economy will tend towards full employment equilibrium. Yet, there is no reason why aggregate demand will necessarily correspond to any supply-side equilibrium. Thus, in the context of ensuring that aggregate savings are brought into line with aggregate investment, to facilitate full employment, the Ricardian equivalence proposition is scarcely relevant (Arestis and Sawyer, 2004a: 74).

A fourth suggestion is that high levels of public debt adversely impact upon economic growth rates. In a highly influential paper, Reinhart and Rogoff (2010) claimed that they had demonstrated an econometric association, such that median growth rates of countries with public debt exceeding 90 per cent of GDP were approximately 1 per cent lower than other nations with lower levels of public debt. They suggested that causes may include the vulnerability to sudden crises in confidence and/or "debt intolerance", as market interest rates begin to rise sharply once debt exceeds certain "tolerance ceilings" (Reinhart and Rogoff, 2010: 577). Unfortunately, this very influential paper contained a number of statistical errors which fatally undermined their findings. Indeed, Herndon et al. (2014) found that, once these were corrected, there was little difference between mean and median growth rates for those countries with above 90 per cent debt levels to other comparative nations. Moreover, even the small association that still remained more probably indicated the effect that low growth caused higher levels of debt rather than the other way around, contrary to the assumption adopted by Reinhart and Rogoff. In other words, their analysis confused correlation with causation (Stiglitz, 2016: 208–210). Furthermore, Herndon et al. (2014: 277) found that growth varied considerably between different countries at each level of public debt amongst the twenty advanced economies included in the initial Reinhart and Rogoff study. Thus, attempts to prove such a link appear to be rather elusive.

A final argument claims that fiscal expansions damage confidence, and may therefore be contractionary, whereas, fiscal austerity, by contrast, creates greater confidence and hence can boost the economy. Essentially, this proposition held that Keynes had completely misunderstood how the economy works and his policy prescriptions produced the opposite of their desired objective. This is a bold claim and it rests upon an argument that begins from a similar starting point as Ricardian equivalence, namely that fiscal expansion ultimately results in fiscal imbalances which have to be corrected either via higher taxation or cuts in public expenditure. Hence, austerity packages that propose reduction in fiscal expenditures reduce the fear of future rises in taxation, thereby boosting consumer confidence and private expenditure. Simultaneously, a more restrictive fiscal policy may facilitate a loosening of monetary policy, as the central bank becomes less concerned about fiscal expansion stimulating inflationary pressures. This, in turn, may facilitate a reduction in interest rates and potentially a depreciation of the value of the exchange rate, both factors having the potential to boost output and investment (Baker et al., 2010: 4; Broadbent and Daly, 2010: 4). This latter point, of course, owes more to the preferences held by central banks rather than anything relating to expectations held by other economic actors (IMF, 2010: 102). Finally, it is proposed that fiscal adjustment reduces the government's demand on the economy's resources, thereby reducing any crowding-out effects and releasing these resources to be better utilised by the private sector.

This view is most closely associated with the work of Alesina and Perotti (1995, 1997), Alesina et al. (1998, 2006) and updated in Alesina and Ardanga (2009), although the case study analysis produced by Giavazzi and Pagano (1990) represented an early statement of what became known as the 'expansionary fiscal contractions hypothesis'. This body of work purported to demonstrate a series of examples where countries that imposed fiscal austerity measures during an economic recession grew more strongly thereafter. Moreover, it was suggested that that this effect was larger if austerity was pursued via reductions in public expenditure rather than through increases in taxation.

The expansionary fiscal contractions hypothesis was rapidly adopted by prominent policymakers across advanced economies. It was adopted enthusiastically in the UK, first in a report by Treasury economists (HM Treasury, 2009) and subsequently in shaping the 2010 emergency budget statement.[2] It influenced a report from the Republican Congressional Joint Economic Committee[3] and it featured prominently in discussions amongst EU policymakers about the future of Eurozone economic policy (Blyth, 2013). Indeed, former President of the ECB Trichet indicated how influential this thesis had become in European policy circles, when he stated in a newspaper interview that:

> It is an error to think that fiscal austerity is a threat to growth and job creation. At present, a major problem is the lack of confidence on the part of households, firms, savers and investors who feel that fiscal policies are not sound and sustainable. In a number of economies, it is this lack of confidence that poses a threat to the consolidation of the recovery. Economies embarking on austerity policies that lend credibility to their fiscal policy strengthen confidence, growth and job creation.[4]

It is notable that the restatement of the expansionary fiscal contractions hypothesis appeared simultaneously alongside the publication of the Reinhart and Rogoff paper on the advantages of cutting public debt. This event coincided with the leading advanced economies reversing their previous stimulus packages and introducing various austerity packages, with predictably negative consequences.[5]

Like the Reinhart and Rogoff hypothesis, however, the Alesina et al. expansionary austerity thesis was not as robust as its advocates might have hoped. For example, detailed examination of a number of the examples of expansionary austerity cited in the various studies produced by Alesina et al. indicate that most did not conform very closely to the original thesis. Only one of the examples cited actually reduced fiscal deficits during a recession and subsequently experienced a period of economic growth, and in that case (Ireland), the recovery was primarily due to devaluation and a loosening of monetary policy (Baker, 2010: 6, 12; Jayadev and Konczal, 2010; Perotti, 2011; Kinsella, 2012). Indeed, Baker (2010: 11) highlights the fact that in a paper by Broadbent and Daly (2010), supporting the expansionary fiscal contractions hypothesis, the results actually indicated that increasing public investment expenditure *increased* economic growth in the short run. Moreover, even the choice of variable composition and statistical method used by Alesina and Ardanga was criticised by the IMF (2010: 94) as representing a "highly imperfect measure of actual policy actions" and biased the results towards the conclusions predicted by the expansionary austerity thesis.

In contrast, two IMF reports found that fiscal consolidation resulted in a contraction of the real economy. The first report estimated that an austerity package equivalent to 1 per cent of GDP typically causes aggregate demand to decline by an equivalent 1 per cent and GDP to fall by around 0.5 per cent within two years (IMF, 2010: 94–99). A subsequent paper found that a fiscal consolidation equivalent to 1 per cent of GDP typically reduced real private consumption by around 0.75 per cent over the following two years, and real GDP by 0.62 per cent (Guajardo et al., 2011). As a result, Stiglitz (2016: 96, 208–209) feels able to conclude that the expansionary austerity conception is fatally flawed and that, rather than stimulating growth, austerity depresses economic activity and thereby confidence.

There is one point on which the critics of an active fiscal policy are correct, and that concerns the fact that fiscal policy is more effective when combined with an accommodative monetary policy (Arestis and Sawyer, 2004b: 129; Freedman et al., 2010). If independent central bankers are determined to frustrate an expansionary fiscal policy, whether due to their individual preferences or as a result of an official mandate given to prioritise low inflation over other objectives in the operation of monetary policy, then fiscal policy will be less effective than could occur if macroeconomic policy was better co-ordinated between the different economic policy agencies.

One result of this may help to explain significant differences in estimates of fiscal multipliers between nations. Hemming, Kell et al. (2002) and Hemming, Mahfouz et al. (2002), for example, calculate these to vary from 0.1 to 3.1. Part of this will arise from the degree to which a country is particularly open to international trade, and hence the degree to which any fiscal stimulus will be subject to leakages, thereby reducing its multiplier effect (Freedman et al., 2009: 4). Nevertheless, another reason for the noted differences in multiplier estimates, particularly between the USA and European nations, is that the former has a central bank with a broader mandate to support employment and growth, whereas the Eurozone has an independent ECB with its sole focus upon securing low rates of inflation.

A Keynesian alternative – functional finance

Keynesian and post-Keynesian schools argue that fiscal policy can have a significant impact on the real economy through its potential to influence both the level and the path of aggregate demand. This, in turn, can influence investment expenditure and thereby the size of the capital stock, together with employment and growth (Arestis, 2009). Since fiscal policy can influence the speed and direction of capital formation, it can influence the economy even in the long run. Of course, it will be less effective in conditions of full employment than where spare capacity exists in the economy, although it is worth noting that, even here, firms prefer to hold some excess capacity and workers can be persuaded to increase numerical flexibility for relatively limited periods of high demand. Fiscal policy, for Keynesians, is a much more potent instrument than interest rate policy in influencing the level of aggregate demand (Arestis and Sawyer, 2010; Angeriz and Arestis, 2009).

The overriding objective of Keynesian fiscal policy is to be measured in terms of its *effects* upon the real economy rather than the maintenance of any arbitrary accounting rule on balanced budgets or 'sound finance' (Lerner, 1943: 469). If the focus of government is to ensure a sufficient level of aggregate demand capable of facilitating full employment, then fiscal policy should be designed to assist this process. Public expenditure is therefore utilised primarily as a macroeconomic policy instrument designed to ensure a sufficient level of aggregate demand, and additional taxation is imposed on those occasions when it is necessary to reduce disposable income and hence consumption, to prevent inflationary pressures.

In the real world, where Say's Law does not hold, there is no certainty that ex ante savings will necessarily equal ex ante investment, and therefore there is no automatic tendency of the economy to move quickly and seamlessly towards full employment. Consequently, there is a clear justification for fiscal policy to close this gap (Keynes, 1936; Kalecki, 1939). If aggregate savings exceed investment, then fiscal expansion should be forthcoming to close the gap and prevent a period of economic slowdown. Similarly, if aggregate investment exceeds savings, then a fiscal surplus should be run to prevent inflationary overheating (Arestis and Sawyer, 2004a: 68). Thus, discretionary fiscal policy, reinforced by automatic stabilisers, can help to smooth short-term fluctuations in economic activity and underpin the desired level of output and employment over the longer term (Arestis and Sawyer, 2013: 145–146). This Keynesian approach to fiscal policy was termed 'functional finance' by Lerner (1943).

One problem with this approach which may arise, given that Keynesians typically anticipate that ex ante savings are more likely to exceed investment rather than vice versa, concerns the possibility that functional finance may result in rising cumulative budget deficits and public debt. This was recognised as a possibility by the originators of the approach. However, they remained relatively unconcerned. Lerner (1943: 475–476) noted that, if public debt were financed from within the nation, then this would merely imply the distributional transfer of resources within society. Moreover, since fiscal deficits would only be required if aggregate savings exceeded investment, then there would, by definition, be sufficient surplus savings available to finance any budget deficit – *quod erat demonstrandum*. In addition, Domar (1944: 822–823) demonstrated that, as long as the growth rate exceeded the rate of interest paid on the level of public debt, then the burden of the debt as a proportion of national income will be reduced, even as the absolute level of debt increases.

An alternative means of equalising aggregate savings and investment at a level sufficient for full employment, proposed by Kalecki (1944), would involve the redistribution of income from capital to labour. Since the propensity to save is higher for those with larger incomes, a progressive redistribution of income would have the effect of reducing private savings and bringing it more into balance with investment. It would thereby ensure sufficient aggregate demand to maintain full employment without the requirement for fiscal deficits.

Keynesian fiscal policy within a reformed EMU

The replacement of the current model of EMU, with a Keynesian ICU alternative, would simplify the use of fiscal policy as the principal instrument with which to counteract asymmetric external shocks, whilst simultaneously making it more effective. This is partly due to the removal of many of the current rules which seek to restrain active fiscal policy measures from operating at national level, but also through the operation of the ICU model itself, as this will provide a more supportive macroeconomic structure. Participating economies will have other outlets to resolve imbalances within their economies, whilst aggregate demand across the ICU should be maintained at a level commensurate with the maintenance of full employment within the currency union.

In the Keynes Plan, the expectation was that fiscal policy would be deployed at national level, to promote full employment within each individual economy, whilst the ICU system would ease this policy goal by seeking to ensure that such macroeconomic management would not be fatally undermined by leakages from the circular flow of income.

For those economies with trade deficits, the ICU would assist through the recycling of idle balances from surplus economies within the currency zone, whether through loans or long-term investment, which should be utilised to increase the capacity and productivity of the recipient economies. If trade deficits were to persist, the ICU would offer the secondary support of currency devaluation to stimulate trade competitiveness.

For surplus economies, they would be encouraged to utilise their surplus balances through stimulating their own economies, if demand deficient, or through making overseas investments across the currency zone. They would additionally benefit from the deficit economies not having to deflate in an attempt to restore trade balance, and in the process reducing the demand for the surplus economy's exports. Thus, the ICU would seek to maintain the conditions within which all participant economies would be more easily able to achieve and sustain their full employment objective.

The criticism that the removal of constraints upon fiscal policy will lead to the free riding of profligate member states upon the rest of the Eurozone, by building up debt denominated in the single currency, would be resolved by the common currency (ICU) Keynesian model, as debt would be denominated in national currencies, and held separate from the common (Euro-bancor) currency.

National or federal fiscal policy

At national level, functional finance benchmarking would operate easily within the ICU. Rather than fiscal policy being constrained by the current SGP and the fiscal compact, these restrictions would play no part in the Keynesian currency union. Instead, fiscal policy should be focused upon securing sufficient aggregate demand to promote a high level of economic activity compatible with full employment. It should not be prevented from achieving this primary goal.

National fiscal policy could also make a significant contribution towards stabilising the EMU zone against the strains imposed through asymmetric shocks, by dealing with the differential consequences for each member state as they begin to impact upon their own national economy, in just the same way as nations who do not take part in single or common currency arrangements. If an asymmetric shock benefits one nation, say Germany, at the expense of another, say Italy, then fiscal policy should tighten in the former and loosen in the latter, to maintain full employment in each individual economy. In the former, this policy reaction would prevent overheating and inflationary pressure, whereas in the latter it would prevent falling output and unemployment. However, the result would also be to stabilise EMU, by ameliorating the magnitude of asymmetric effects that would otherwise disrupt the common currency zone. The ICU structure would additionally ease this stabilising effect, through the maintenance of conditions favourable to full employment across the union as a whole, and enabling any longer term shifts in economic conditions to be dealt with through currency peg revaluation as and when necessary.

There are a number of reasons, however, that would suggest that national fiscal policy could be augmented by a degree of fiscal federalism introduced across the ICU, and which could assist in long-run stabilisation (De Grauwe and Vanhaverbeke, 1993: 112–125; Hein, 2013: 350). Indeed, one proposal of this nature has been developed, using the attractive designation of a 'Full Employment, Growth and Stability Pact', thereby neatly differentiating the proposed objectives of a Keynesian approach from the existing EMU neo-liberal model (Arestis, 1999: 9–10; Arestis et al., 2001).

The operation of the ICU would lessen the need for fiscal federalism in the currency union quite considerably compared to the current position. However, a common currency zone would still inevitably facilitate the development of regional spillovers or externalities, where citizens in other member states benefit from burdens borne ultimately by citizens in another participating nation. As a consequence, the introduction of federal fiscal transfers would more equitably share the burdens inherent in the stabilisation of the common currency zone as a whole (Rompuy et al., 1993: 112–113). In effect, this could act as an inter-regional public insurance scheme that could redistribute income from 'favourably shocked' to 'adversely shocked' regions to prevent an 'unlucky' area bearing a disproportionate financial burden. It would, moreover, reinforce political and social solidarity throughout all participating member states (Bayoumi and Masson, 1995). Given that the Eurozone currently encompasses severe examples of divergent economic performance, with unemployment in 2015 varying from 2.5 per cent in the regions of Freiburg and Niederbayen (both Germany) to 34 per cent in Melilla and 31.5 per cent in Andalucia (both Spain), a federal scheme to share burdens in this way would be both politically as well as economically advantageous.[6]

Fiscal federalism could be pursued through an expansion in the EU budget, as envisioned by the MacDougall Report, although their prediction that this could encompass between 20 per cent and 25 per cent of Eurozone GDP in a mature EMU, would necessitate the transfer of whole swathes of national expenditure to federal control (MacDougall, 1977). This might prove politically problematic, particularly since not all EU member states are currently members of the Eurozone, and therefore might not wish (or be permitted) to join the ICU. It would, moreover, hamper the operation of national forms of fiscal policy which would retain an essential role in securing full employment in each individual country under the common currency model. Consequently, it might prove to be more efficacious to consider introducing an automatic stabiliser operating at supranational level, to specifically target federal fiscal expenditures on those areas of the Eurozone where shocks have an adverse impact.

Variants of what might be termed a European Federal Transfer Scheme (EFTS) have been proposed which would be triggered by a change in the real economy which indicated that one part of the currency union had been adversely affected by an external shock, compared to the union as a whole. Indicators could include a specified rise in unemployment or reduction in growth. It would operate by drawing resources from those areas of the currency union which have been more favourably impacted by the external shock. Careful design can generate an EFTS which is a more efficient stabiliser than existing tax and transfer systems which developed to fulfil alternative objectives. For example, one proposal, made by Italianer and Vanheukelen (1993: 500), envisaged a EFTS achieving a similar degree of stabilisation as the fiscal federalism of the USA for an average annual cost equivalent to only 0.23 per cent of EU GDP. Similarly, a second proposal calculated the average annual cost at between 0.17 per cent and 0.86 per cent of EU GDP for securing an 18 per cent stabilisation of an initial shock, depending upon precise estimates of the elasticity of output loss associated with higher unemployment (Whyman, 2010).

Fiscal federalism has been criticised due to its cost, in terms of the significant transfers required to ensure a sufficient level of stabilisation is achieved (Whyman, 2010; Degryse, 2012; Bellofiore, 2013: 509). Perhaps paradoxically, therefore, it may be more likely to secure the necessary level of support for this type of bold initiative if it formed part of a more ambitious growth and full employment promoting economic strategy, combined with solidaristic social policy at the heart of an alternative conception of EMU as outlined in this book (Grahl and Teague, 2013: 690). The common currency model would make precisely such a prioritisation and thus is more likely to be supported by those interests within the EU who desire this type of alternative conception of the European project.

Conclusion

This chapter has sought to demonstrate how a Keynesian form of active fiscal policy could be utilised to stabilise a common currency zone more effectively than the current Eurozone model. In the absence of nation states conforming to the standards of a neo-classical textbook, where economies rapidly and automatically move from one natural equilibrium to another, there would appear to be an a priori case for a broader role for active fiscal policy to stabilise a common currency arrangement. This could be assigned to national or federal levels, but would most likely benefit from the combination of the two different but complementary approaches.

The key difference, however, between the Keynesian and the current Eurozone approach to the use of fiscal policy concerns the need to remove constraints upon its ability to promote that level of economic activity sufficient to secure the full employment of resources within each individual economy, and thereby across the common currency zone as a whole. The failure to incorporate this broader role for active fiscal policy within the EMU model will almost inevitably lead to further current account imbalances and thus resulting in either deflation in peripheral member states or increasing conflict leading to pressure for a fracturing of the currency union (Kaldor, 1971).

The ICU alternative form of EMU would facilitate the use of fiscal policy through providing a supportive macroeconomic framework within which fiscal measures would not have to do all the heavy lifting of pursuing full employment within the national economy whilst simultaneously seeking to stabilise the currency zone as a whole. Thus, rather than trying to bolt on a more active fiscal policy to the present Eurozone, as certain theorists have suggested, with the consequent tension between the different elements of the current approach, its replacement by an ICU model of EMU would provide a mutually beneficial environment where the ICU framework and fiscal measures would complement and reinforce each other, thereby improving the effectiveness of each.

Notes

1 http://ec.europa.eu/economy_finance/economic_governance/sgp/legal_texts/index_en.htm (accessed 21 November 2017).
2 http://webarchive.nationalarchives.gov.uk/20130129110402/www.hm-treasury.gov.uk/junebudget_speech.htm (accessed 21 November 2017).
3 www.speaker.gov/sites/speaker.house.gov/files/UploadedFiles/JEC_Jobs_Study.pdf (accessed 21 November 2017).
4 www.ecb.europa.eu/press/key/date/2010/html/sp100713.pdf?39a6e4938418767f5e407762cd5f1260 (accessed 21 November 2017).
5 www.nybooks.com/articles/2013/06/06/how-case-austerity-has-crumbled/?pagination=false&printpage=true (accessed 21 November 2017).
6 Eurostat data on unemployment by NUTs 2 regions. Available via: http://ec.europa.eu/eurostat/tgm/table.do?tab=table&init=1&language=en&pcode=tgs00010&plugin=1 (accessed 21 November 2017).

Bibliography

AFME (2011), 'Proposals for Common Eurozone Sovereign Issuance', *Discussion Paper*, Association for Financial Markets in Europe, London.

Alesina, A. and Ardanga, S. (2009), 'Large Changes in Fiscal Policy: Taxes Versus Spending', *NBER Working Paper* No. 15434, Cambridge, MA. Available via: www.nber.org/papers/w15438.pdf.

Alesina, A., Ardagna, S. and Trebbi, F. (2006), 'Who Adjusts and When? The Political Economy of Reform', *IMF Staff Papers*, 53 Special Issue. Available via: www.imf.org/External/Pubs/FT/staffp/2006/03/pdf/alesina.pdf.

Alesina, A. and Perotti, R. (1995), 'Fiscal Expansion and Adjustments in OECD Economies', *Economic Policy*, 10(21): 207–247.

Alesina, A. and Perotti, R. (1997), 'Fiscal Adjustments in OECD Countries: Composition and Macroeconomic Effects', *IMF Staff Papers*, 44(2): 210–248.

Alesina, A., Perotti, R. and Tavares, J. (1998), 'The Political Economy of Fiscal Adjustments', *Brookings Papers on Economic Activity*, 1: 197–266.

Angeriz, A. and Arestis, P. (2009), 'The Consensus View on Interest Rates and Fiscal Policy: Reality or Innocent Fraud?', *Journal of Post Keynesian Economics*, 31(4): 567–586.

Arestis, P. (1999), 'The Independent European Central Bank: Keynesian Alternatives', *Jerome Levy Economics Institute Working Paper* No. 274.

Arestis, P. (2007), 'What Is the New Consensus in Macroeconomics?', in Arestis, P. (Ed.), *Is There a New Consensus in Macroeconomics?* Houndmills, Palgrave, Basingstoke.

Arestis, P. (2009), 'Fiscal Policy Within the "New Consensus Macroeconomics" Framework', in Creel, J. and Sawyer, M. (Eds.), *Current Thinking on Fiscal Policy*, Palgrave, Basingstoke, 6–27.

Arestis, P., McCauley, K. and Sawyer, M. (2001), 'An Alternative Stability Pact for the European Union', *Cambridge Journal of Economics*, 25(1): 113–130.

Arestis, P. and Sawyer, M. (1998), 'Keynesian Policies for the New Millennium', *Economic Journal*, 108(446): 181–195.

Arestis, P. and Sawyer, M. (2000), 'Deflationary Consequences of the Single Currency', in Baimbridge, M., Burkitt, B. and Whyman, P.B. (Eds.), *The Impact of the Euro: Debating Britain's Future*, Macmillan, London.

Arestis, P. and Sawyer, M. (2004a), 'On Fiscal Policy and Budget Deficits', *Intervention: Journal of Economics*, 1(2): 65–78.

Arestis, P. and Sawyer, M. (2004b), *Re-Examining Monetary and Fiscal Policy for the 21st Century*, Edward Elgar, Cheltenham.

Arestis, P. and Sawyer, M. (2010), 'The Return of Fiscal Policy', *Journal of Post Keynesian Economics*, 32(3): 327–346.

Arestis, P. and Sawyer, M. (2013), *Economic and Monetary Union Macroeconomic Policies: Current Practices and Alternatives*, Palgrave, Basingstoke.

Baimbridge, M. and Whyman, P.B. (2008), *Britain, the Euro and Beyond*, Ashgate, Aldershot.

Baimbridge, M. and Whyman, P.B. (2015), *Crisis in the Eurozone*, Palgrave, Basingstoke.

Baker, D. (2010), *The Myth of Expansionary Fiscal Austerity*, Center for Economic and Policy Research, Washington, DC. Available via: http://cepr.net/documents/publications/austerity-myth-2010-10.pdf.

Barro, R. and Gordon, D. (1983), 'Rules, Discretion, and Reputation in a Model of Monetary Policy', *Journal of Monetary Economics*, 12(1): 101–121.

Bayoumi, T. and Eichengreen, B. (1993), 'Shocking Aspects of European Monetary Integration', in Torres, F. and Giavazzi, F. (Eds.), *Adjustment and Growth in the European Monetary Union*, Cambridge University Press, Cambridge, 193–229.

Bayoumi, T. and Masson, P.R. (1995), 'Fiscal Flows in the United States and Canada: Lessons for Monetary Union in Europe', *European Economic Review*, 39: 253–274.

Bellofiore, R. (2013), 'Two or Three Things I Know About Her: Europe in the Global Crisis and Heterodox Economics', *Cambridge Journal of Economics*, 37(3): 497–512.

Bibow, J. (2015), 'Making the Euro Visible: The Euro Treasury Plan', *Levy Economics Institute Working Paper* No. 842. Available via: www.levyinstitute.org/pubs/wp_842.pdf.

Bieler, A. (2006), *The Struggle for a Social Europe: Trade Unions and EMU in Times of Global Restructuring*, Manchester University Press, Manchester.

Bird, G. and Mandilaras, A. (2012), 'Will Europe's Fiscal Compact Help Avoid Future Economic Crises?', *University of Surrey Discussion Papers in Economics*, DP 12/12. Available via: www.surrey.ac.uk/sites/default/files/DP12-12.pdf.

Blyth, M. (2013), *Austerity: The History of a Dangerous Idea*, Oxford University Press, Oxford.

Broadbent, B. and Daly, K. (2010), 'Limiting the Fall-Out From Fiscal Adjustments', *Goldman Sachs Global Economics Paper* 195. Available via: www.irisheconomy.ie/GSGEP195.pdf.

Burkitt, B., Baimbridge, M. and Whyman, P. (1996), *There Is an Alternative*, Nelson & Pollard, Oxford.

Buti, M., Franco, D. and Ongena, H. (1997), *Budgetary Policies During Recessions: Retrospective Applications of the Stability and Growth Pact to the Post-War Period*, European Commission, Brussels.

Carlin, W. and Soskice, D. (1990), *Macroeconomics and the Wage Bargain*, Oxford University Press, Oxford.

Claessens, S., Mody, A. and Vallee, S. (2012), 'Paths to Eurobonds', *IMF Working Paper* No. WP/12/172.

Copelovitch, M., Frieden, J. and Walter, S. (2016), 'The Political Economy of the Euro Crisis', *Comparative Political Studies*, 48(7): 811–840.

Cwik, T. and Wieland, V. (2010), 'Keynesian Government Spending Multipliers and Spillovers in the Euro Area', *European Central Bank Working Paper* No. 1267. Available via: www.ecb. europa.eu/pub/pdf/scpwps/ecbwp1267.pdf?5ed52b5ab649fecb6236f72c090252f3.

De Grauwe, P. and Mosen, W. (2009), 'Gains for All: A Proposal for a Common Eurobond', *CEPS Commentaries*. Available via: http://aei.pitt.edu/11091/1/1823[1].pdf.

De Grauwe, P. and Vanhaverbeke, W. (1993), 'Is Europe an Optimum Currency Area?', in Masson, P.R. and Taylor, M.P. (Eds.), *Policy Issues in the Operation of Currency Unions*, Cambridge University Press, Cambridge, 111–129.

Degryse, C. (2012), 'The New Economic Governance', *ETUI Working Paper* No. 14, Brussels.

Delpla, J. and von Weizsäcker, J. (2010), 'The Blue Bond Proposal', *Bruegel Policy Brief* 2010/03.

Domar, E.D. (1944), 'The Burden of the Debt and the National Income', *American Economic Review*, 34(4): 798–827.

ECB (2005), *Monthly Bulletin*, March, ECB, Frankfurt.

EC Commission (1990), 'One Market, One Money', *European Economy*, 44, Office for the Official Publications of the European Communities, Luxembourg.

Eichengreen, B. (1992), 'Is Europe an Optimum Currency Area?', in Borner, S. and Grubel, H. (Eds.), *The European Community After 1992: Perspectives From the Outside*, Macmillan, London, 138–161.

Elmendorf, D. and Furman, J. (2008), *If, When How: A Primer on Fiscal Stimulus*, The Brookings Institution, Washington, DC. Available via: www.brookings.edu/wp-content/uploads/ 2016/06/0110_fiscal_stimulus_elmendorf_furman.pdf.

Emerson, M., Gros, D., Italianer, A., Pisani-Ferry, J. and Reichenbach, H. (1992), *One Market, One Money: An Evaluation of the Potential Benefits and Costs of Forming an Economic and Monetary Union*, Oxford University Press, Oxford.

EU Commission (2011), *Green Paper on the Feasibility of Introducing Stability Bonds* [COM 818], European Commission, Brussels.

EU Commission (1992), *Treaty on European Union*, Office for the Official Publications of the European Communities, Luxembourg.

EU Commission (1996), *The Community Budget – 1996 Edition*, Office for the Official Publications of the European Communities, Luxembourg.

EU Commission (1997), 'The Stability and Growth Pact', *InfEuro*, Office for the Official Publications of the European Communities, Luxembourg.

EU Commission (1998), *Financing the European Union: Commission Report on the Operation of the Own Resources System*, Office for the Official Publications of the European Communities, Luxembourg.

EU Commission (2004a), *General Budget of the European Union for the Financial Year 2004*, Office for the Official Publications of the European Communities, Luxembourg.

EU Commission (2004b), *Allocation of 2003 EU Operating Expenditure by Member State*, Office for the Official Publications of the European Communities, Luxembourg.

EU Commission (2011), *Green Paper on the Feasibility of Introducing Stability Bonds* [COM 818], European Commission, Brussels.

EU Commission (2012), *New Crisis Management Measures to Avoid Future Bank Bailouts*, Press Release, June, European Commission, Brussels.

Feldstein, M. (1997), 'The Political Economy of an European Economic and Monetary Union: Political Sources of an Economic Liability', *Journal of Economic Perspectives*, 11(4): 23–42.

Freedman, C.M., Kumhof, D., Laxton, D. and Lee, J. (2009), 'The Case for a Global Stimulus', *IMF Staff Papers*, SPN/09/03, International Monetary Fund, Washington, DC. Available via: www.imf.org/external/pubs/ft/spn/2009/spn0903.pdf.

Freedman, C.M., Kumhof, D., Laxton, D., Muir, D. and Mursula, S. (2010), 'Global Effects of Fiscal Policy During the Crisis', *Journal of Monetary Economics*, 57(5): 506–526.

Friedman, M. (1956), 'The Quantity Theory of Money: A Restatement', in Friedman, M. (Ed.), *Studies in the Quantity Theory of Money*, University of Chicago Press, Chicago, 1–21.

Friedman, M. (1962), *Capitalism and Freedom*, University of Chicago Press, Chicago.

Galbraith, J.K. (1997), 'Time to Ditch the NAIRU', *Journal of Economic Perspectives*, 11(1): 93–108.

Giavazzi, F. and Pagano, M. (1990), 'Can Severe Fiscal Contractions Be Expansionary? Tales of Two Small European Countries', in Blanchard, O. and Fischer, S. (Eds.), *NBER Macroeconomics Annual 1990*, MIT Press, London, 75–111.

Giovannini Group (2000), *Co-Ordinated Public Debt Issuance in the Euro Area: Report of the Giovanni Group*. Available via: http://ec.europa.eu/economy_finance/publications/publication6372_en.pdf.

Goodhart, C.A.E. and Smith, S. (1993), 'Stabilisation', in 'The Economics of Community Public Finance', *European Economy*, Reports and Studies, 5: 419–455.

Grahl, J. and Teague, P. (2013), 'Reconstructing the Eurozone: The Role of EU Social Policy', *Cambridge Journal of Economics*, 37(3): 677–692.

Gros, D. and Micossi, S. (2009), 'A Bond-Issuing EU Stability Fund Could Rescue Europe', *Europe's World Discussion Paper* 12. Available via: http://europesworld.org/2009/02/01/a-bond-issuing-eu-stability-fund-could-rescue-europe/.

Guajardo, J., Leigh, D. and Pescatori, A. (2011), 'Expansionary Austerity: New International Evidence', *IMF Working Paper* No. WP/11/158. Available via: www.imf.org/external/pubs/ft/wp/2011/wp11158.pdf.

Hein, E. (2013), 'Finance-Dominated Capitalism and Redistribution of Income: A Kaleckian Perspective', *Levy Economics Institute of Bard College Working Paper* No. 746.

Hemming, R., Kell, M. and Mahfouz, S. (2002), 'The Effectiveness of Fiscal Policy in Stimulating Economic Activity: A Review of the Literature', *IMF Working Paper* No. 02/208, International Monetary Fund, Washington, DC. Available via: www.imf.org/external/pubs/ft/wp/2002/wp02208.pdf.

Hemming, R., Mahfouz, S. and Schimmelpfennig, A. (2002), 'Fiscal Policy and Economic Activity During Recessions in Advanced Economies', *IMF Working Paper* No. 02/87, International Monetary Fund, Washington, DC.

Herndon, T., Ash, M. and Pollin, R. (2014), 'Does High Public Debt Consistently Stifle Economic Growth? A Critique of Reinhart and Rogoff', *Cambridge Journal of Economics*, 38(2): 257–279.

HM Treasury (2009), *International Examples of Spending Consolidations*. Available in partially redacted form via: www.hm-treasury.gov.uk/foi_fiscal_consolidation_010210.htm.

IMF (2010), *World Economic Outlook: Recovery, Risk and Rebalancing*, IMF, Washington, DC. Available via: www.imf.org/external/pubs/ft/weo/2010/02/pdf/text.pdf.

Italianer, A. and Vanheukelen, M. (1993), 'Proposals for Community Stabilisation Mechanisms: Some Historical Applications', in 'The Economics of Community Public Finance', *European Economy, Reports and Studies*, 5: 495–510.

Jayadev, A. and Konczal, M. (2010), 'The Boon Not the Slump: The Right Time for Austerity', *Economics Faculty Working Paper* No. 26, University of Massachusetts, Boston, MA. Available via: http://scholarworks.umb.edu/econ_faculty_pubs/26.

Kaldor, N. (1971), 'The Dynamic Effects of the Common Market', *New Statesman*, 12 March, 59–91.

Kalecki, M. (1939), *Essays in the Theory of Economic Fluctuations*, Russell and Russell, New York.

Kalecki, M. (1944), 'The White Paper on Employment Policy', *Bulletin of the Oxford University Institute of Statistics*, 6(8): 137–144.

Kenen, P.B. (1969), 'The Theory of Optimum Currency Areas: An Eclectic View', in Mundell, R. and Swoboda, A. (Eds.), *Monetary Problems of the International Economy*, University of Chicago Press, Chicago.

Kenen, P.B. (1995), 'What Have We Learned From the EMS Crises?', *Journal of Policy Modelling*, 17(5): 449–461.

Keynes, J.M. (1923), *A Tract on Monetary Reform*, Macmillan, London.

Keynes, J.M. (1936), *The General Theory of Employment, Interest and Money*, Macmillan, Basingstoke, 1973 edition.

Kinsella, S. (2012), 'Is Ireland Really the Role Model for Austerity?', *Cambridge Journal of Economics*, 36(1): 223–235.

Krugman, P. (2012), 'Revenge of the Optimum Currency Area', *NBER Macroeconomics Annual*, 27(1): 439–448. Available via: www.nber.org/chapters/c12759.pdf.

Kydland, F.E. and Prescott, E.C. (1977), 'Rules Rather Than Discretion: The Time Inconsistency of Optimal Plans', *Journal of Political Economy*, 85(3): 473–499.

Lane, P.R. (2006), 'The Real Effects of European Monetary Union', *Journal of Economic Perspectives*, 20(4): 47–66.

Lane, P.R. (2012), 'The European Sovereign Debt Crisis', *Journal of Economic Perspectives*, 26(3): 49–68.

Layard, R. and Nickell, S. (1985), 'The Causes of British Unemployment', *National Economic Institute Review*, 111: 62–85.

Lerner, A. (1943), 'Functional Finance and the Federal Debt', *Social Research*, 10(1): 38–51.

MacDougall, D. (1977), *The Role of Public Finance in the European Communities*, Office for the Official Publications of the European Communities, Luxembourg.

Masson, P.R. (1996), 'Fiscal Dimensions of EMU', *Economic Journal*, 106(437): 996–1004.

Mathers, A. (2007), *Struggling for a Social Europe: Neo-Liberal Globalisation and the Birth of a European Social Movement*, Ashgate, Aldershot.

McKinnon, R. (1963), 'Optimum Currency Areas', *American Economic Review*, 53(4): 717–725.

Meerpol, M. (1998), *Surrender: How the Clinton Administration Completed the Reagan Revolution*, The University of Michigan Press, Michigan, 2000 edition.

Monperrus-Veroni, P. and Saraceno, F. (2006), 'Whither Stability Pact? An Assessment of Reform Proposals', in Mitchell, W., Muysken, J. and Van Veen, T. (Eds.), *Growth and Cohesion in the European Union: The Impact of Macroeconomic Policy*, Edward Elgar, Cheltenham, 32–56.

Muellbauer, J. (2011), 'Resolving the Eurozone Crisis: Time for Conditional Eurobonds', *CEPR Policy Insight* 59.

Mundell, R.A. (1961), 'A Theory of Optimum Currency Areas', *American Economic Review*, 51(4): 657–665.

Neville, J.W. (2000), 'Can Keynesian Policies Stimulate Growth in Output and Employment?', in Bell, S. (Ed.), *The Unemployment Crisis in Australia: Which Way Out?* Cambridge University Press, Cambridge, 149–174.

Oates, W.E. (1972), *Fiscal Federalism*, Harcourt-Brace and Jovanovich, New York.

OECD (1986), *Flexibility in the Labour Market*, OECD, Paris.

Palley, T.I. (1998), *Plenty of Nothing: The Downsizing of the American Dream and the Case for Structural Keynesianism*, Princeton University Press, Princeton, NJ.

Perotti, R. (2011), 'The "Austerity Myth": Gain Without Pain', *NBER Working Paper* No. 17571. Available via: www.nber.org/papers/w17571.

Reinhart, C. and Rogoff, K. (2010), 'Growth in a Time of Debt', *American Economic Review: Papers and Proceedings*, 100(2): 573–578.

Rompuy, P.V., Abraham, F. and Heremans, D. (1993), 'Economic Federalism and the EMU', in 'The Economics of EMU – Background Studies', *European Economy*, 44, 109–135.

Setterfield, M., Gordon, D.V. and Osberg, L. (1992), 'Searching for a Will O'Wisp: An Empirical Study of the NAIRU in Canada', *European Economic Review*, 36(1): 119–136.

Stiglitz, J.E. (2016), *The Euro and Its Threat to the Future of Europe*, Allen Lane, London.

von Hagen, J. (1993), 'Monetary Union and Fiscal Union: A Perspective From Fiscal Federalism', in Masson, P.R. and Taylor, M.P. (Eds.), *Policy Issues in the Operation of Currency Unions*, Cambridge University Press, Cambridge, 264–296.

Weber, A.A. (1991), 'EMU and Asymmetries and Adjustment Problems in the EMS', in 'The Economics of EMU', *European Economy*, Special Edition 1, 44(1): 187–207.

Whyman, P.B. (2006), *Third Way Economics*, Palgrave, Basingstoke.

Whyman, P.B. (2010), 'Stabilising Economic and Monetary Union in Europe: The Potential for a Semi-Automatic Stabilisation Mechanism', in Tavidze, A. (Ed.), *Progress in Economics Research, Volume 18*, Nova Science Publishers, Hauppauge, NY, 1–26.

5 Breathing life into the European Social Model

> The outstanding faults of the economic society in which we live are its failure to provide for full employment and its arbitrary and inequitable distribution of wealth and incomes.
>
> (Keynes, 1936: 372)

Introduction

One distinctive feature of the model of regional integration, advanced by the EU, concerns the creation of a social dimension (*espace social européen*) or European Social Model (ESM). Although not featuring particularly prominently within the early trade-dominated incarnation of the EU, the concept of creating a social Europe developed through initiatives such as the Social Action Programme in the 1970s, the Charter of Fundamental Social rights of Workers in 1989, and were enshrined in the Treaty on European Union and the Amsterdam Treaty (Hantrais, 2007: 2–3; Whyman et al., 2012: 1–2, 212–220). The Treaty on European Union (EU Commission, 1992) committed the EU to:

> promote economic and social progress and a high level of employment and to achieve balanced and sustainable development, in particular through the creation of an area without internal frontiers, through the strengthening of economic and social cohesion and through the establishment of economic and monetary union, ultimately including a single currency in accordance with the provisions of this Treaty.

The ESM has been proposed as a means of counter-balancing some of the less desirable consequences likely to arise from the unfettered operation of free market forces (Bean et al., 1998). The concept of a 'social Europe' is typically counterpoised against the neo-liberal, free market 'Anglo-Saxon' model, in that it is an expression of the solidaristic ideal that society should not abandon the weaker members of society or those who do not succeed as well in life as other members of the community (Hemerijck and Ferrera, 2004). In essence, the ESM was intended to ensure at least a partial de-commodification of labour, which would empower employees and was predicted to encourage the development of work relationships based upon trust and loyalty, rather than the market nexus (Esping-Andersen, 1990). This was considered to be increasingly important in the dynamic knowledge-based sectors of the economy and was thought likely to encourage investment in human capital (Teague, 1997).

In contrast to neo-liberal theorists, this conception of social protection advances the proposition that a trade-off between social equity and economic efficiency is not inevitable, and, rather, the former can enhance efficiency through reducing poverty, thereby reducing constraints upon participation in economic activity (de Neubourg and Casonguay, 2006: 180). Indeed, in the long term, there does appear to be some evidence that reductions in inequality may have a positive impact upon economic growth developments (Wilkinson and Pickett, 2009). Of course, social expenditure must be financed, and this may lead to higher costs for employees or firms, but the net impact upon productivity depends upon how policy design enhances incentives to invest in human capital and the extent to which training opportunities are available (de Neubourg and Casonguay, 2006: 201–202). Hence, generous social security systems do not *necessarily* result in lower labour market participation rates and higher unemployment if this is supplemented by active labour market measures (de Groot et al., 2006: 175).

The ESM is, furthermore, considered to embrace an employment aspect, whereby European citizen rights and wellbeing is promoted through the enhancement of social partnership between employers and employees – typically, though not exclusively, through trade unions. Social partnership is intended to promote interaction between employers and employees, and in turn, to facilitate positive-sum solutions to mutual problems. The emphasis upon the inclusion of workers and their unions in the working of the economy is intended to facilitate 'voice' rather than 'exit', and in turn, facilitate co-operation in adapting to change, superior morale resulting in enhanced productivity and lower employee turnover, and finally the prevention of low-skill, low investment competitive alternatives stimulates productive investment and innovation (Streeck, 1992: 5; Hutton, 1994; Coates, 1999: 654–655). The introduction of European Works' Councils, in large trans-national corporations operating within the EU economies, demonstrates an interest in facilitating consultation and enhancing micro-level flexible adaptation. Furthermore, universal employee protection whilst at work forms a core element of the ESM (Strange, 1997).

In part, this proposition is a little naïve, in that it assumes away the inevitable conflicts and differences of interest which exist in the work relationship, and indeed, in most forms of human interaction, when scarce resources come up against unlimited (or at least, less scarce) demands. This lies at the heart of the economic problem, discussed by students in the first few days of studying the subject. It also exists in a workplace where, to take the most obvious example, there is a diversification of interests in determining reward systems, when it is extremely difficult to decide upon what is fair and what rewards effort, whilst shareholders require payment for their risk capital and firms require resources to reinvest for future production. Differences of interest are, therefore, inevitable. However, that is not to say that there are not certain areas where mutual interest can be pursued, and where positive-sum (not zero-sum) solutions are possible. Thus, it is in the interests of all concerned that firms are competitive and profitable if achieved through new ideas and/or innovation, but not if the same achievements are gained through reducing wages and/or increasing work intensity.

The broadening of collective bargaining across member states rather than remaining a predominantly national preserve – so-called Euro-bargaining – reinforces social partnership as a component of wider integration objectives (Peters, 1995: 321; Berthold and Fehn, 1998: 530). Indeed, it would be difficult to achieve an equalisation of conditions and rewards for a car worker in Italy and Germany without some form of European sectoral bargaining. Similarly, in the absence of negotiations to establish common working conditions and/or a gradual equalisation of pay rates, it is unlikely that workers in the agricultural sectors of Poland and Lithuania will have mutual identification of common interests with their equivalent figures in the UK or Sweden. Hence, for advocates of this approach, it would appear to be an essential means of augmenting the single European market into providing a benefit for all employees rather than just business interests.

The ETUC (European Trade Union Confederation) remains, not surprisingly, a strong advocate of this approach. However, European employer organisations remain equally hostile to this development. Moreover, the persistence of rivalries between unions, whether due to organisational competition, religious or ideological reasons, might equally impair co-ordinated bargaining across the entire European market (Turner, 1996: 330). Nevertheless, a large body of the literature has indicated that co-ordinated wage formation produces a superior macroeconomic flexibility in real wages and hence industrial adjustment to external shocks to the economy (Bruno and Sachs, 1985; Calmfors and Driffill, 1988; Rowthorn and Glyn, 1990).

The ESM has proven particularly popular amongst social democratic and trade union constituencies (Strange, 1997; Ross and Martin, 1999; Whyman, 2002, 2007). Indeed, it has been suggested that ESM measures may have been advocated specifically to gain support from these constituencies for the neoliberal variant of European integration (Moss, 2005: 11). It has the potential to provide a means of evading the "crisis of national trade unionism" that Hoffmann (2002: 143–144) suggested would result from globalisation and the deepening of European integration. At least, it would if the basic tenants of the ESM are compatible with those of the model of EMU adopted to form the basis for this further economic integration within Europe.

There are, however, a number of problems with the development of the ESM, not the least of which is the fact that it is poorly defined (Vaughan-Whitehead,

2003: 3). This may actually be an advantage for those seeking to use its potential adoption as a means of broadening a coalition of support for deeper economic integration. Thus, for example, it is possible to present the ESM as a variant of the post-war German *social market*. This approach has combined a successful, competitive market economy with generous welfare provision, labour protection and an exceptional vocational training system producing skilled workers of sufficient quantity and quality, thereby rectifying the corporate tendency to under-invest in skill formation (Teague, 1997).

There have been a few attempts made to codify the ESM. One such attempt, made by the EU, arose out of the summit in Nice, in 2000. This suggested that the ESM derived from a "common core of values" relating to the provision of a high degree of social protection, the recognition of the importance of dialogue between social partners and the necessity to promote social cohesion as essential elements within the process of European integration (EU, 2000). This was developed further in the Amsterdam Treaty, which identified five broad areas that together would constitute the basis for the ESM. These are (Ball, 2001; Adnett and Hardy, 2005: 7):

1   Promoting employment
2   Reorganising work
3   Combating social exclusion
4   Mainstreaming gender equality
5   Consolidation, compliance and enforcement of social legislation.

These principles were intended to promote social policy objectives at the European level. Moreover, the ESM incorporated the requirement for social partner involvement in the development of these measures; a requirement intended to promote 'voice' within the European economy. It additionally embraced trade unions as a legitimate social partner and counterpoint to organised business organisations, thereby promoting employee involvement in relevant aspects of working life at both local and super-national level. This provided a new legitimate role for unions to fulfil, during a time period when organised labour was being increasingly marginalised in many European nations (Whyman, 2002).

Yet, alongside attempts to de-commodify labour and provide a minimum level of social standards, the ESM has also been viewed as a means of promoting a 'level playing field' for competition across the single market, through the creation of a broad equivalence in labour standards (Adnett and Hardy, 2005: 8). Indeed, even the strengthening of 'voice' within the European economy has been portrayed as a means of stimulating investment and productivity (Streeck, 1992: 5). Thus, the ESM initiative has found itself to be the focus of a divergence of definition, between those, on the one hand, who perceive it to deliver a kinder form of European economy, characterised by de-commodified labour and with social harmonisation raising the standards for all across Europe, whereas others view it as a means of utilising social and labour market policy as a means to enhance competition within the single market whilst enhancing international competitiveness beyond.

Tensions between neo-liberal EMU and a social Europe

The coexistence of a comprehensive ESM alongside a neo-liberal version of EMU is problematic for a number of reasons.

Heterogeneity

First, there remains a high fragmentation of social policy within, and between, EU member states, with common initiatives to provide social protection restricted to covering only the lowest common denominator (Whyman, 2001). This may suggest that European regulation may only be possible for non-contentious issues, where nations share common interests and goals, such as health and safety matters (Keller and Sorries, 1997: 93).

This divergence between member states has, moreover, been exacerbated by the more recent waves of enlargement (Whyman et al., 2012). Post-enlargement, GDP per capita (measured in purchasing power standards)[1] ranges from 40 per cent of the EU(15) average in Latvia, to 210 per cent in Luxembourg, whereas the degree of inequality experienced within the new member states (NMS) tends towards outlier positions when compared with the majority of other EU nations (Vaughan-Whitehead, 2003: 53; EU Commission, 2006: 2,43). This can be seen in Figure 5.1, where NMS tend to group amongst the most and the least equal amongst EU nations. Hence, enlargement has increased the diversity of experience in terms of income distribution across the EU. It is anticipated that this range of relative affluence will diminish over time due to the 'catch-up' process – although this depends upon a large number of factors, including the adoption of an appropriate economic policy framework, and is by no means as automatic as many commentators are apt to suggest (FitzGerald, 2006). As a result, a greater disparity of social inequality, both within and between member states, presents a significant challenge to the ESM (Whyman et al., 2012: 256).

In terms of hourly monthly earnings, workers in the NMS, together with Portugal and Greece, receive the lowest rates of remuneration within the EU (see Figure 5.2). To a large extent, this reflects differences in productivity across the EU. However, it has additionally made pan-European wage bargaining more difficult, given the diversity of wages between member states that this would need to take into consideration.

The industrial relations climate within the NMS is, on the most part, markedly different from the experience within the EU(15) nations, due to the fragmentation and hence weakness of the social partners (particularly trade unions). Bargaining typically occurs at workplace than sectoral level as in the majority of the more established member states (Vaughan-Whitehead, 2003: 244; EIRO,

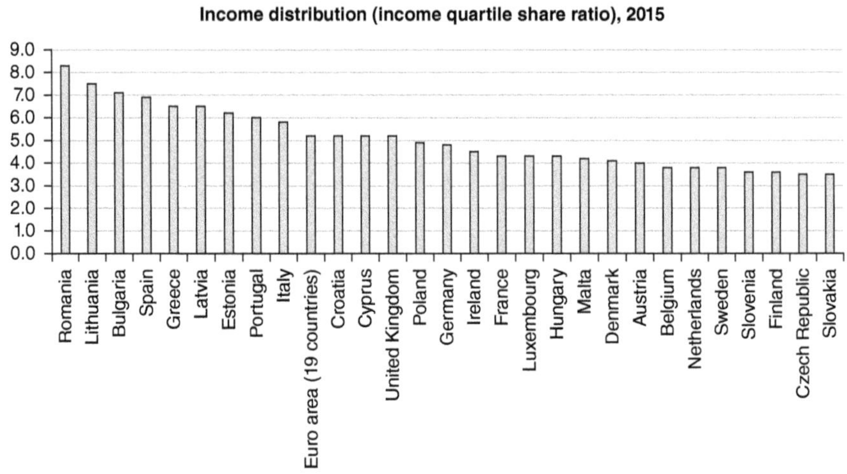

Income distribution (income quartile share ratio), 2015

Figure 5.1 Income distribution (income quintile share ratio), 2015

(Source: Eurostat, accessed on 18 September 2017, via: http://appsso.eurostat.ec.europa.eu/nui/setup-Downloads.do).

2005). Enlargement has, therefore, increased the diversity of employment conditions and industrial relations arrangements. This is likely to frustrate the creation of a comprehensive bargaining structure being established across the single European labour market, as envisaged by European trade unions, at least in the short run. Similarly, the fragmentation of bargaining situations and low levels of trade union membership effectively denies the majority of workers in the NMS the opportunity to exercise their collective voice in meaningful wage negotiations.

Social protection, moreover, tends to receive a lower prioritisation amongst many NMS when compared to EU(15) countries. Whereas the EU average expenditure on social protection is around 27 per cent, the average for the post-command economy new member states was less than 20 per cent, whilst corresponding figures for Malta were only marginally higher and those for Cyprus were remarkably low at around 8 per cent of GDP (Vaughan-Whitehead, 2003: 117). There is also a greater reliance upon means testing than the universal benefits more typical of the more established EU member states (Vaughan-Whitehead, 2003; Eatwell, 2000: 149).

Part of this difference may, in fact, derive from the substantial economic and social costs experienced by those new member states transitioning from command to market economies during the 1990s (Kregel et al., 1992; ILO, 1995; Andor and Summers, 1998). This may have precipitated a retrenchment of social measures in reaction of difficult economic circumstances. Or, alternatively, it

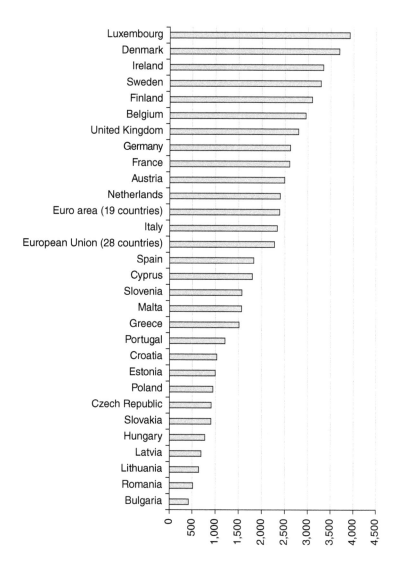

Figure 5.2 Average monthly earnings (€), 2014

(Source: Eurostat, accessed on 18 September 2017, via: http://appsso.eurostat.ec.europa.eu/nui/setup-Downloads.do).

may reflect a more straightforward adoption of neo-liberal doctrines by the transition economies, whereby a higher level of social expenditure is perceived as weakening incentives and potentially damaging macroeconomic objectives of low inflation and interest rates; themselves contributing towards higher rates of economic growth (Vaughan-Whitehead, 2003: 116).

Not all recorded variance in experience across the EU stems from enlargement, however, as a review of the unemployment and under-employment figures testify (Figures 5.3 and 5.4). Whilst Croatia, Cyprus and Slovakia have higher than average unemployment rates, other NMS tend towards some of the lowest rates across the EU. However, it is more established member states, such as Greece, Spain, Italy and Portugal, that record particularly poor performance in terms of open unemployment and hidden under-employment rates. This fact is repeated when considering the incidence of youth unemployment, which varies considerably across the EU, between 7.1 per cent in Germany and 10.8 per cent in the Netherlands, to 44.4 per cent in Spain and 47.3 per cent in Greece.

The variance in labour market performance, across the EU, makes it more difficult to develop a set of comprehensive labour laws and regulations which could establish common minimum standards for the single European marketplace. The same is true for social policy, as different levels of unemployment, inequality and social expenditure, effectively frustrate the creation of a common minimum safety net across the whole of the EU.

Dependence upon EMU performance

A second problem with the ESM is that its viability depends upon the economic success of the European economy. This is both in terms of this generating the resources necessary to finance social measures and generous forms of

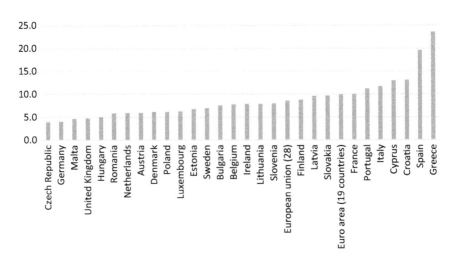

Figure 5.3 Unemployment rates (%) in 2016 between those aged 15–74

(Source: Eurostat, accessed on 18 September 2017, via: http://appsso.eurostat.ec.europa.eu/nui/setup-Downloads.do).

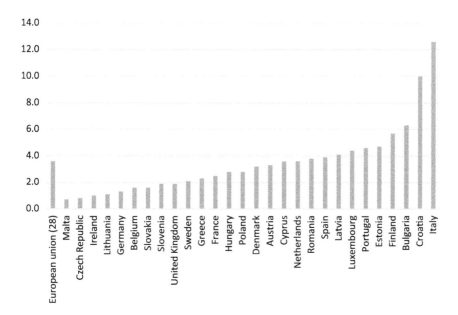

Figure 5.4 Individuals available but not seeking work as a % of the active population, 2016

(Source: Eurostat, accessed on 18 September 2017, via: http://appsso.eurostat.ec.europa.eu/nui/setup-Downloads.do).

labour market protection, but also because economic failure would place a considerable strain upon social interventions intended to mollify negative consequences. Given that the core EU member states are members of the Eurozone, the ESM is at least partially dependent upon the success of the particular model of EMU chosen by the EU to lie at the heart of the European integration process, whilst it is simultaneously intended to moderate some of the distributional consequences that arise from the operation of the single currency.

There are some obvious issues raised in this respect. The most immediate concerns the restrictions placed upon the generosity of social provision due to the requirement to adhere to the fiscal rules outlined in the previous chapter. As national social policy expenditure is constrained by rules on budget deficits and public debt, initially introduced by the Maastricht Treaty and subsequently tightened by both the Stability and Growth Pact (SGP) and most recently the fiscal compact, the social wage is being squeezed in many member states (EU Commission, 1992; Bouget, 2003: 679).

The current conception of EMU places additional hurdles in the path of the pursuit of aspects of the ESM. For example, the removal of barriers to financial flows and increasing integration of European capital markets has led to an increasing dominance of capital markets over bank credit financing, resulting in a shift in corporate control and governance across much of the European economic space. This creates a further potential rift with the ESM ideal, as labour market strategy, intended to protect workers from at least certain market vagaries, would conflict more clearly with this new focus upon market-driven corporate strategy, whilst conceptions of employee participation in corporate decision-making and/or economic democracy, would appear less likely to be accommodated (Watson, 2006). Moreover, the economic architecture surrounding EMU would appear to encourage the consideration of wages and social protection as costs rather than benefits, likely to undermine the competitiveness of a participating nation unable to restore competitive advantage through devaluation and/or changes in monetary policy due to the single currency.

A single currency framework also creates problems for those individual member states who become less competitive for one reason or another. This may be caused by an internal shock or an external event that impacts differently upon this nation than its neighbours. The former could include inflationary wage developments or asset bubbles of the type preceding the recent financial crisis. Examples of the latter could include a significant shift in the oil price or the cost of particular raw materials used in its dominant industries or, indeed, a change in the demand for its most significant export categories. Irrespective of the cause, the current version of single currency precludes these economies from using instruments such as monetary or exchange-rate policy to restore competitiveness, and hence governments must consider further reductions in fiscal expenditure, with the result of deflating the economy, and/or ensuring wage moderation (Holland, 1995; Teague, 1998: 119–120). As alternative instruments previously used to adjust the competitiveness of an industry (or economy) are no longer available, member states will depend upon the ability of wage formation systems to deliver wages consistent with international competitiveness (Hyman, 2005: 15). This, in turn, creates further tensions for a system of social protection consistent with the logic inherent within a neoliberal version of a single currency (Moss, 2005: 12).

In circumstances of a loss of national competitiveness, it is likely that additional pressure will be placed upon pay negotiators to ensure that, *in aggregate*, wages grow in line with productivity. This may be more easily achieved through a form of co-ordinated wage bargaining, occurring at central or industrial level, where all parties can internalise the inflationary implications of their decisions (Whyman, 2006: 126–128). The Netherlands, Germany and Ireland, for example, have sought to promote wage bargaining moderation through national or sector-level pay bargaining structures during the transition towards, and membership of, EMU (Teague, 1998: 119–120). Nevertheless, it is unlikely that the ETUC has remained such a strong advocate of this approach in order to bind union negotiators to maintain an almost permanent wage moderation, irrespective of labour market conditions or the distributional balance and level of inequality within each member state. Hence, any requirement for increased wage discipline, which may arise due to the operation of EMU and the resultant pressure to maintain national competitiveness through squeezing the social wage, will inevitably exacerbate difficulties for the trade union movement (Melitz, 1997; Pissarides, 1997).

Supranational ESM measures could counter this squeeze on social protection, but this would require the introduction of common levels of support for economies as diverse as Germany and Denmark, on the one hand, and Romania and Latvia on the other. However, it is not simply a matter of EU enlargement having exacerbated the divergence of labour market regulation and social protection across the EU as a whole. Indeed, even the wealthier and more successful member states have questioned the affordability of generous social measures due to the pressures of globalisation and the need to maintain international competitiveness. In Germany, for example, non-wage labour costs are seen as a prime factor contributing to what became described as the *Standortfrage*, namely the questioning of whether Germany had become uncompetitive as a production location (Flockton, 1998: 79). The former chief economist and member of the Executive Board of the ECB, Issing (2000), reflected these concerns when he suggested that the logic of EMU required greater labour cost variability between EU member states to reflect differences in productivity. In the absence of a parallel shift to harmonise upwards productivity levels across the EU, the levelling-up of minimum wages and other labour standards would cause a cost crisis for less productive member states and may undermine the economic viability of many industries in the less productive economies.

The reunification of the former East Germany with West Germany provides a salutary lesson in the dangers inherent in currency unification without first adequately considering the relative levels of productivity and wages in the two economies. In this case, a decision was taken to unify the East Germany currency, the Ostmark, into the Deutschemark, at a one-to-one ratio for prices, wages, pensions and relatively small currency holdings. Larger savings and housing loans were converted at a slightly less generous ratio of 2:1, and currency holdings acquired shortly before unification, and therefore primarily for speculative reasons, were converted at a ratio of 3:1. This was despite the East German economy being only about half as productive as their Western neighbours. This efficiency gap was masked by the fact that East German employees had an average 20 per cent longer working hours than their West German counterparts, and were paid only around one-third average West German wage rates (Lumley, 1996: 26). As a result, wage equalisation without a corresponding increase in productivity severely reduced East German competitiveness as, in 1991, gross wages in manufacturing in the East averaged 138 per cent of net value-added. Predictably, manufacturing collapsed under the twin cost pressure of wage rises and exchange-rate appreciation, with output falling by 67 per cent in the first year after unification and leading to 25 per cent of the entire labour market losing their jobs (Akerlof et al., 1991; Sinn and Sinn, 1992). A year after monetary union, only 44 per cent of the previous 9 million workforce of East Germany remained in the same employment relationship (Buechtemann and Schupp, 1992: 95–97, 102–104).

Moreover, all of this took place despite the generous fiscal transfer system employed in that case (Buechtemann and Schupp, 1992; Horn and Zwiener, 1992). Between 1991 and 2003, it has been estimated that West Germany transferred between 4–5 per cent of its GDP to the former East German provinces (Hunt, 2006), whilst more recent calculations have placed the total transfer at perhaps €1.3 trillion.[2] This represented more than half of the initial East German GDP.

In the current model of EMU, there is no similar generous fiscal transfer scheme being contemplated nor is this level of generosity likely to be politically feasible in the near future. Thus, the ESM by itself, and without support provided by a more accommodating macroeconomic policy framework within which to operate, would be unlikely to achieve the type of levelling-up that most adherents of the ESM approach would expect it to deliver. Indeed, it is more likely that any unification of social protection measures at levels pertaining to less productive member states would imply a dramatic series of cuts in social expenditure in wealthier EU nations.

To the extent that persistent differences in wage levels and a 'social gap' in terms of differing levels of social protection and labour regulations reflect a variance in factor endowments and productivity levels, then these differences may be justified on the basis of economic necessity in order to maintain a nation's international competitiveness. However, where they are retained when productivity levels rise, this can give rise to a nation gaining an unfair competitive advantage through reliance upon lower social and/or labour standards – what is often termed 'social dumping'. Unless checked, this could result in 'beggar-thy-neighbour' strategies employing the downgrading of social policy measures rather than employing options discouraged by EU membership, including devaluation and/or industrial subsidies, thus causing 'race to the bottom'. Yet, this is a difficult relationship to estimate, as is clear from some of the early attempts to measure the extent of the problem (Adnett, 1995; Leibfried and Pierson, 1995; EU Commission, 2006).

Neo-liberal critique of ESM

One final problem in relation to the development of an ESM is the increasingly vocal neo-liberal critique of welfare states, labour regulation and centralised wage bargaining as causes of 'Eurosclerosis' (Lawrence and Schultz, 1987). Generous welfare provision has been criticised as being responsible for a decline in economic performance (Feldstein, 1974, 1976; Lindbeck et al., 1994; Agell, 1996). Increases in taxation to fund higher levels of government transfers are suggested to reduce work incentives, increase the rate of natural unemployment and depress economic dynamism, whilst social security reduces personal savings rates, thereby reducing the stock of capital and hence national income. Job security legislation is claimed to produce hysteresis, where an individuals' duration of unemployment is negatively related to their probability of getting a job (Lawrence and Schultz, 1987). Indeed, the ECB's former board member and chief economist, Issing, blamed the poor performance of the Euro on "the adverse impact of minimum wage and employment protection legislation", which can only be overcome by a "comprehensive programme of structural reform".[3]

The evidence on these points is rather mixed and support for the neo-liberal critique of the ESM approach is rather elusive. Welfare expenditure, for example, is not simply a drain upon the vitality of the private sector, but acts as an automatic stabiliser which will maintain the level of demand for these same private firms and prevent the economy from drifting into recession. Social insurance, similarly, may enable workers to take greater risks in their working lives which may produce greater returns for society as a whole (Korpi, 1985, 1996; Barr, 1992). Moreover, when utilising the appropriate mix of active labour market policies and co-ordinated wage formulation, corporatism tends to present an improved unemployment: inflation trade-off (Jackman et al., 1990: 483; Rhodes, 1992: 29).

Incomplete ESM

Given the problems, it is perhaps not such a surprise that the results, to date, derived from the ESM measures have been rather modest, with the possible exception of health and safety measures (Martin and Ross, 1999: 319). Thus, the current form of social dimension being constructed across the EU is, arguably, a *minimalist* (or weak) version of a fully fledged system of social protection of the kind operated idealised in discussion of the ESM (Keller and Sorries, 1997: 93; Whyman, 2001, 2007). Indeed, it is a moot point whether the subsidiarity principle informs and reinforces the considerable fragmentation in this area of policy, or is actually an ex post facto attempt to recognise and provide a narrative to justify the divergence in social and employment matters across the EU member states.

Critics of the current position have argued that it has "retarded [the] advancement of European-level political rights", alongside the "almost complete absence of a European system of industrial citizenship" as indicating that there is little reason to anticipate these initiatives will prove particularly successful (Streeck, 1992: 218–219). Similarly, Barnard and Deakin (1997: 131) have described the current approach as an "eclectic body of employment law", whilst others claim the approach has a "hollow core" (Leibfried, 1994: 246; Leibfried and Pierson, 1995). Consequently, whilst unfair to dismiss such achievements as meaningless, or treat the social dimension as though it were a complete and coherent approach, it is nevertheless grossly insufficient for the EU Commission to portray this as a distinct ESM (see Table 5.1).

The current failure of the EU to develop a truly comprehensive version of ESM does not, of course, imply that it may do so in the future. Indeed, the conception of the social dimension of European integration is contested and a focal point for social and political struggle (Adnett and Hardy, 2005: 1; Hyman, 2005: 10; Bieler, 2006; Mathers, 2007). Nevertheless, it highlights some of the

Table 5.1 A comparison between a fully developed ESM and the current EU 'social dimension'

	EU social dimension	European Social Model
Welfare state		
Type	Minimalist	Comprehensive
Coverage	Safety net	Universal
Replacement ratio	Low	High
Association with labour market	Re-commodification	De-commodification
Response to globalisation	Competitive – improve labour market skills	Protective – social citizenship requires non-market income source to make effective choices
Industrial relations		
Recognition of collective bargaining	Patchy	High/comprehensive
Corporatist	Diverse – some member states deregulated wage formation, whilst others rely upon social contracts to secure budget cuts	Established – facilitates superior inflation: employment trade-off
Euro-level IR	Minimum – EWC, consultation only	Developed – framework bargaining between federal-level social partners
Labour regulation	Minimum – complements single market; over-regulation impedes competitiveness	Fundamental – basis of social accord, combining industrial adjustment with employee protection

(Source: Table adapted by the author from Baimbridge and Whyman [2008: 169]).

difficulties in developing a comprehensive ESM alongside the current model of neo-liberal EMU.

The desire to remain competitive within a neo-liberal model of EMU would appear to be the motivation behind a regressive wave of welfare reform that has taken place across much of the EU, as macroeconomic policy becomes increasingly constrained and unable to shield national labour market institutions and social protection arrangements (Hemerijck and Ferrera, 2004: 248). Moreover, the influence of the ECB has been used to reinforce wage constraint and welfare retrenchment in pursuit of international competitiveness (Stiglitz, 2016: 154–155). Thus, critics have identified the introduction of EMU as the "Trojan horse" (Featherstone, 2004: 226) that has enabled the implementation of neo-liberal economics throughout the EU, which undermines the fundamental characteristics of any progressive ESM (McNamara, 1998). Trapped within the economic foundations of EMU, it may be difficult to perceive the ESM being able to thrive or even survive in any meaningful sense (Hodge and Howe, 1999). In essence, it is quite plausible that the objectives of the ESM and EMU may be incompatible (Adnett and Hardy, 2005: 26).

Flexicurity

The flexicurity strategy was advanced by the EU as a means of seeking to find a way in which employment (but not job) protection could be reconciled with the perceived need to introduce greater flexibility in labour markets (OECD, 2010: 181–190; Martin and Scarpetta, 2012). Firms would be better able to adapt rapidly to changing demand conditions and take advantage of new opportunities to innovate (EC, 2007: 3–4; OECD, 2013: 66–68). However, there is evidence that too much liberalisation of labour market protection, and the creation of dualistic or segmented labour markets, can generate negative consequences not only in distributional but also dampening economic efficiency (Schettkat, 2003; OECD, 2013: 67–68). Thus, flexicurity was conceived as an integrated approach to advance flexibility whilst retaining a significant element of security in the labour market (EC, 2007: 4–5).

There is a certain degree of ambiguity concerning both the meaning and operationalisation of flexicurity, rather as there has been with the definition of the ESM as a whole (Burroni and Keune, 2011). One aspect of this relates to the differences between internal and external flexicurity. The former involves increasing the flexible utilisation of employees within an organisation, whether through temporal flexibility (i.e. part-time or flexitime working) or functional flexibility (i.e. team working or multi-skilling to perform multiple roles). The latter, by contrast, concerns the use of active labour market policy to secure the correct levels of skills within the labour force relative to the skills needs of employers, whilst simultaneously enhancing the ability of individuals to move more easily between different jobs. The Commission has tended to focus primarily upon external flexicurity (Heyes, 2013: 72). It has, moreover, recognised that divergence in employment rights, industrial relations and social protection regimes across the EU means that flexicurity would need to be introduced from different initial starting points, and therefore there would be an absence of uniform adoption across all member states (EC, 2007: 19–20; Heyes, 2013: 73). Nevertheless, the approach was conceived as having four main components (EC, 2007: 5). These are:

1   Flexible and reliable contractual arrangements – preventing the creation of dualistic labour markets, comprised of 'insiders' and 'outsiders', through 'modern' labour legislation, collective agreements and work organisation;
2   Comprehensive life-long-learning – ensuring continual adaptability of the labour force and the social inclusion of vulnerable groups;
3   Effective labour market policies – designed to assist individuals to adapt to rapidly changing labour market opportunities, thereby shortening unemployment duration and facilitating transition to new jobs;
4   Modern social security systems – providing sufficient levels of social provision (i.e. income support, pensions, healthcare) to encourage labour market mobility and work–life balance.

To this could be added a fifth element, namely that flexicurity was intended to embrace the active involvement of social partners to ensure that all stakeholders should benefit (EC, 2007: 8, 18).

Despite being advanced as a means of securing increased competitiveness, through enhancing the flexibility of EU economies without abandoning key elements of social protection, the flexicurity initiative has tended to emphasise the former (flexibility) rather than the latter (employment protection). Part of the reason for this has been the reaction to the recent financial crisis and the austerity measures promoted by the EU as a means of reducing fiscal deficits in line with the SGP and fiscal compact requirements (Heyes, 2013: 74). The impact of these measures has had a detrimental impact upon social dialogue. Indeed, the 'Athens Manifesto', presented by the European Trade Union Confederation (ETUC) at its 2011 ETUC Congress, indicated how concerned that organisation had become over this shift in the EU's approach on these matters that it announced its commitment to fight against austerity, unemployment, inequality, precarious work and cuts in pay and social security (ETUC, 2011).

The problems inherent in the flexicurity concept, however, are more fundamental. In its current form, the approach is insufficient, because the desire to preserve a significant proportion of social protection and employment regulation conflicts with the imperatives of a neo-liberal EMU, in much the same way as there exists tension between the provisions of EMU for the ESM as a whole. Ultimately, therefore, flexicurity is likely to struggle to persevere against the imperatives to reduce costs through squeezing wages, social provision and working conditions, in order to retain or regain competitiveness within a single currency regime. It will be increasingly forced to focus upon external market-conforming labour market flexibility (Heyes, 2013), and hence fail to counter the slide towards using social policy to promote competition states rather than enhance employment security (Cerny, 1990, 1997). Then use of flexible labour markets and the promotion of industrial adjustment to global change are market-conforming and in direct conflict with the ESM approach, as universal welfare provision is replaced by education, training and mobility measures designed to enhance productivity and increase employment levels. It would re-commodify individuals, albeit provide them with the opportunity to develop more skills and therefore be better placed in the labour market. This has prompted certain theorists to conclude that, operating within the confinement of a neo-liberal variant of EMU, a social Europe is "an impossible dream" (Whyman et al., 2012: 320–321).

How might a Keynesian approach differ?

A Keynesian version of EMU would provide a much more conducive environment within which a comprehensive ESM could not only become established, but thereafter make a positive contribution to the common currency model. Rather than seeking to operate counter to many of the economic fundamentals of a neo-liberal regime, the ESM would be in a position to reinforce the Keynesian EMU approach.

In order to understand how this change could occur, it is useful to consider a simple economics textbook example of how neo-classical and Keynesian economic schools of thought view the interaction between the labour market and the economy as a whole. Since this example is intended to be illustrative, and meant to be accessible to those who are less familiar with a series of equations utilised to explain these relationships, diagrammatic form will suffice.

Neo-classical economics holds that the labour market is comprised of multiple sellers of their labour and firms that wish to purchase labour to make their goods or deliver services. In order to simplify the model, it is typically assumed that all workers have homogenous skills and are therefore interchangeable in different employment situations. In practice, this is not of course the case, and hence rather than one generic labour market there would be multiple markets for different skill sets and job requirements. Nevertheless, on the basis of this simplified model, an equilibrium price of labour, or real wage rate (W/P_e), will ensure that as many workers as wish to work at this prevailing rate will find employers wishing to hire at this wage cost (N_e). If wages were lower, there would be more employers seeking low-cost labour than individuals wishing to work at this low wage, whereas at a rate higher than the equilibrium, there would be more workers willing to enter the labour market than firms willing to hire. Thus, the equilibrium wage clears the market. All those who do not have a job are voluntarily unemployed, because they have chosen not to enter the market at a lower wage rate. This equilibrium position is illustrated in the top left-hand corner of the series of Figure 5.5.

In order to ascertain what level of national income or GDP will be produced by the aggregate supply of labour in the economy as a whole, the equilibrium quantity of labour (N_e), determined in the labour market, is transformed by the aggregate production function (the second part of this diagram). This production function indicates how inputs into production – such as land, capital and, in this case, labour – determine outputs, dependent upon the prevailing level of technological advance. In this case, N_e workers will produce a total output worth Y_e, which equates to the supply-determined level of equilibrium national income of GDP in the economy. This aggregate supply of labour is vertical, in the bottom segment of this diagram, because there is no role for aggregate demand to cause more than a temporary movement away from the labour-market-determined level of employment. It is often termed a natural rate of unemployment. If aggregate demand was increased, it would simply result in higher prices (inflation), thus leaving the natural rate and real wage rate in the labour market unchanged (see the neo-classical diagram in Figure 5.6).

In the neo-classical model, therefore, it is easy to understand why the introduction of an ESM is problematic, since social protection and employment regulation are viewed as raising the cost of employing labour. Unless compensated by a commensurate decline in the wage rate, ESM measures would be viewed by neo-liberal economists as causing fewer workers to be demanded

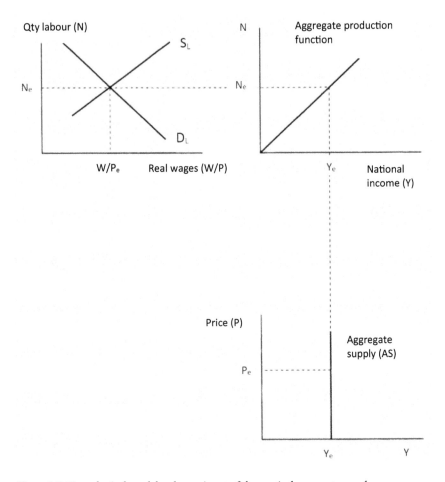

Figure 5.5 Neo-classical model – determinant of the vertical aggregate supply curve

by employees, whilst a reduced level of equilibrium labour will cause aggregate supply to shift to the left, and the economy suffer a decline in national income. According to this simple neo-classical approach, the most obvious means of reducing unemployment and restoring competitiveness in an economy would be to reduce employment regulation, social policy and/or the real wage.

The Keynesian economic school of thought rejects this approach. It argues that it is demand that determines the aggregate level of employment in the economy. Aggregate demand is closely related to the degree of capacity pertaining in an economy at any given time, and this, in turn, is associated with encouraging industrial investment, enhancing productivity and acting as a significant determinant of the level of unemployment (Rowthorn, 1995; Arestis

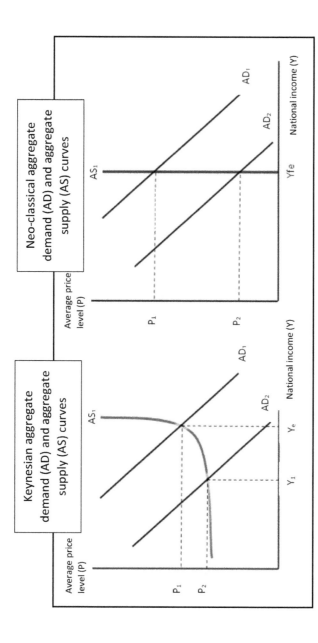

Figure 5.6 Comparison of Keynesian and neo-classical aggregate demand (AD) and aggregate supply (AS) curves

and Mariscal, 1997: 191; Dow, 1998: 369; Baddeley, 2003). Therefore, aggregate demand is a major factor influencing the supply curve of available labour, thereby affecting numerical flexibility, whilst the buoyancy of the economy may influence the replacement ratio, impacting upon the degree of wage flexibility, together with the willingness of employees to accept certain types of non-standard employment and so forth.

The Keynesian approach recognises the reality of demand-deficient unemployment, whereby individuals who wish to work, are unable to do so not because they are unwilling to work at the prevailing wage rate, but because there is insufficient demand in the economy to encourage employers to want to hire these workers. Accordingly, the aggregate supply curve is shown to be more horizontal than vertical, in Figure 5.2, across a range of different levels of national income, signifying that changes in aggregate demand can cause employment levels to change across this range. It is only as the economy approaches full employment that the Keynesian aggregate supply curve becomes near vertical. Even here, however, there is room for higher demand to squeeze additional production out of an existing workforce, through overtime working and other forms of temporal flexibility.

Perusal of these two very different ways of understanding the economy highlights the reason why a Keynesian economic framework is much more conducive to the establishment of an ESM, since employment regulation and social policy can play a useful role in sustaining a sufficient level of aggregate demand to maintain full employment. The Keynesian approach would additionally foster the development of a true flexicurity, combining both micro- and macro-flexibility with decent levels of social provision and employment protection. Micro-flexibility would promote the flexible utilisation of workers within an organisation, intended to realise mutual gains for both employer and employee (Whyman and Petrescu, 2014). Macro-flexibility would involve the promotion of co-ordinated or centralised wage bargaining to support a sufficient level of aggregate demand to secure full employment without over-stimulating inflation (Meidner, 1983: 15; Holmlund, 1988).

Co-ordinated bargaining can only effectively operate within a general Keynesian approach; otherwise social partners are caught in a trilemma, whereby they cannot promote superior macroeconomic gains such as higher levels of employment at low levels of inflation, whilst simultaneously seeking greater wage levelling and a more equitable distribution of national income between wage and capital shares (Swenson, 1989). In the current new monetarist Eurozone framework, social pacts are reduced to moderating wages in the expectation that lower wages will result in higher levels of employment, irrespective of the regressive distributional consequences (Fajertag and Pochet, 1997; Glyn, 1995: 55). Yet, trade unions required to accede to these arrangements are not in control over whether this increase in employment actually materialises.

In a Keynesian framework, with aggregate employment levels determined by demand factors, co-ordinated bargaining can play a more significant role, as trade unions can press for the type of more progressive distributional framework envisaged by most advocates of the ESM. The advocates of the Rehn-Meidner (Swedish) model demonstrated how the combination of a post-Keynesian macroeconomic framework, co-ordinated solidaristic wage bargaining and active labour market policy, can produce favourable macroeconomic policy goals (Whyman, 2003: 35–52). The introduction of an ESM within a Keynesian common currency framework is mutually reinforcing, since aggregate demand management may similarly impact upon the continued optimality of the wage bargaining institutions and patterns of bargaining (Calmfors and Driffill, 1988; Iversen, 1999).

The combination of micro- and macro-flexibility would, additionally, limit the opportunity and attractiveness for employers to adopt a cost-minimisation production strategy and therefore incentivise firms for invest in human capital development (Streeck, 1992: 264). The literature further identifies potential gains through reductions in labour turnover, thereby realising further gains from skills training investment, together with the promotion of structural change and reducing industrial conflict (Calmfors and Driffill, 1988; Rowthorn and Glyn, 1990).

Conclusion

The Keynesian (ICU) model of EMU provides fertile soil into which the ESM can properly flourish. The maintenance of full employment, through a more active management of aggregate demand and complementing the operation of the ICU ensuring the recirculation of idle balances and preventing the formation of substantive and persistent imbalances within an ICU zone, can provide this supportive framework. The maintenance of a high level of demand within the ICU eases public expenditure constraints and thereby has the potential to facilitate investment in social policy programmes. Likewise, initiatives to promote labour market regulation would be facilitated by a European economy at full employment. By contrast, the current new monetarist version views social and labour market policy as primarily the means to squeeze inflation and thereby retain international competitiveness and it is, therefore, incompatible with the full implementation of the ESM.

For those progressive political parties and trade unions whose support for EMU is at least partly conditional upon the completion of a comprehensive version of the ESM, this is a troubling conclusion. Consequently, those progressive forces within the EU should be minded to weigh the relative merits of the current system against the potential of the Keynesian ICU alternative in terms of which approach would appear more able to deliver their vision of a social Europe. Were they to engage in such a deliberation, it would seem self-evident which conclusion that they would ultimately reach. It would then simply depend upon whether they would be prepared to struggle for this more progressive version of EMU or whether Europe would remain locked within a more volatile, neo-liberal system.

Notes

1 Purchasing power standards are calculated by Eurostat in order to compare the economic performance of countries by controlling for price level differences. Purchasing power parities are used as a means of converting economic indicators into purchasing power standards rather than denoted in national currencies.
2 Reuters. (2009). 'Study Shows High Cost of German Reunification: Report', 7 November, available via: www.reuters.com/article/us-germany-wall-idUSTRE5A613B20091107.
3 Blair, A. (2000), 'Managing Change: A National and International Agenda of Reform?', speech given at the World Economic Forum, Davos, Switzerland, 28 January.

Bibliography

Adnett, N. (1995), 'Social Dumping and European Economic Intervention', *Journal of European Social Policy*, 5(1): 1–12.

Adnett, N. and Hardy, S. (2005), *The European Social Model: Modernisation or Evolution?* Edward Elgar, Cheltenham.

Agell, J. (1996), 'Why Sweden's Welfare State Needed Reform', *Economic Journal*, 106(439): 1760–1771.

Akerlof, G., Rose, A., Yellen, Y. and Hessenius, H. (1991), 'East Germany in From the Cold: The Economic Aftermath of Currency Union', *Brookings Papers on Economic Activity*, 1: 1–87.

Andor, L. and Summers, M. (1998), *Market Failure: Eastern Europe's 'Economic Miracle'*, Pluto, London.

Arestis, P. and Mariscal, I. (1997), 'Conflict, Effort and Capital Stock in UK Wage Determination', *Empirica*, 24(3): 179–193.

Baddeley, M.C. (2003), *Investment: Theories and Analysis*, Palgrave, Basingstoke.

Baimbridge, M. and Whyman, P.B. (2008), *Britain, the Euro and Beyond*, Ashgate, Aldershot.

Ball, S. (2001), 'The European Employment Strategy: The Will But Not the Way?', *Industrial Law Journal*, 30(4): 353–374.

Barnard, C. and Deakin, S. (1997), 'European Community Social Law and Policy: Evolution or Regression?', *Industrial Relations Journal*, European Annual Review: 131–153.

Barr, N. (1992), 'Economic Theory and the Welfare State: A Survey and Interpretation', *Journal of Economic Literature*, 30: 741–803.

Bean, C., Bentolila, S., Bertola, G. and Dolado, J. (1998), *Social Europe: One For All?* Centre for Economic Policy Research, London.

Berthold, N. and Fehn, R. (1998), 'Does EMU Promote Labour-Market Reforms?', *Kyklos*, 51(4): 509–536.

Bieler, A. (2006), *The Struggle for a Social Europe*, Manchester University Press, Manchester.

Bouget, D. (2003), 'Convergence in the Social Welfare Systems in Europe: From Goal to Reality', *Social Policy & Administration*, 37(6): 674–693.

Bruno, M. and Sachs, J.D. (1985), *Economics of World-Wide Stagflation*, Blackwell, Oxford.

Buechtemann, C.F. and Schupp, J. (1992), 'Repercussions of Reunification: Patterns and Trends in the Socio-Economic Transformation of East Germany', *Industrial Relations Journal*, 23(2): 90–106.

Burroni, L. and Keune, M. (2011), 'Flexicurity: A Conceptual Critique', *European Journal of Industrial Relations*, 17(1): 75–91.

Calmfors, L. and Driffill, J. (1988), 'Bargaining Structure, Corporatism and Macroeconomic Performance', *Economic Policy*, 6: 13–62.

Cerny, P.G. (1990), *The Changing Architecture of Politics: Structure, Agency and the Future of the State*, Sage, London.

Cerny, P.G. (1997), 'The Deregulation and Re-Regulation of Financial Markets in a More Open World', in Cerny, P.G. (Ed.), *Finance and World Politics Markets, Regimes and States in the Post-Hegemonic Era*, Edward Elgar, Aldershot.

Coates, D. (1999), 'Models of Capitalism in the New World Order', *Political Studies*, 47: 643–660.

de Groot, H., Nahuis, R. and Tang, P. (2006), 'The Institutional Determinants of Labour Market Performance: Comparing the Anglo-Saxon Model and a European-Style Alternative', in Mitchell, W., Muysken, J. and Van Veen, T. (Eds.), *Growth and Cohesion in the European Union: The Impact of Macroeconomic Policy*, Edward Elgar, Cheltenham, 157–179.

de Neubourg, C. and Castonguay, J. (2006), 'Enhancing Productivity: Social Protection as Investment Policy', in Mitchell, W., Muysken, J. and Van Veen, T. (Eds.), *Growth and Cohesion in the European Union: The Impact of Macroeconomic Policy*, Edward Elgar, Cheltenham, 180–205.

Dow, J.C.R. (1998), *Major Recessions: Britain and the World, 1920–1995*, Oxford University Press, Oxford.

Eatwell, J. (2000), 'Unemployment: National Policies in a Global Economy', *International Journal of Manpower*, 21(5): 343–373.

EC [European Commission] (2007), *Towards Common Principles of Flexicurity: More and Better Jobs Through Flexibility and Security*, COM (2007) 359, Official Publications of the European Communities, Luxembourg. Available via: http://eur-lex.europa.eu/legal-content/EN/TXT/PDF/?uri=CELEX:52007DC0359&from=EN.

EIRO [European Industrial Relations Observatory] (2005), *Changes in National Collective Bargaining Systems Since 1990*, EIRO, Dublin.

Esping-Andersen, G. (1990), *The Three Worlds of Welfare Capitalism*, Polity, Cambridge.

ETUC [European Trade Union Confederation] (2011), *The Athens Manifesto*, ETUC, Brussels. Available via: www.etuc.org/a/8747.

EU (2000), 'European Social Agenda', in *Presidency Conclusions: Nice European Council Meeting*, 7–9 December, EN SN 400/00, ADD1 (Annex 1).

EU Commission (1992), *Treaty on European Union*, Office for the Official Publications of the European Communities, Luxembourg.

EU Commission (2006), 'Enlargement, Two Years After: An Economic Evaluation', *European Economy – Occasional Papers No. 24*, EU Commission, Luxembourg.

Fajertag, G. and Pochet, P. (Eds.) (1997), *Social Pacts in Europe*, European Trade Union Institute, Brussels.

Featherstone, K. (2004), 'The Political Dynamics of External Empowerment: The Emergence of EMU and the Challenge to the European Social Model', in Martin, A. and Ross, G. (Eds.), *Euros and Europeans: Monetary integration and the European model of society*, Cambridge University Press, Cambridge, 226–247.

Feldstein, M.S. (1974), 'Social Security, Induced Retirement and Aggregate Capital Accumulation', *Journal of Political Economy*, 82: 905–926.

Feldstein, M.S. (1976), 'Temporary Layoffs in the Theory of Unemployment', *Journal of Political Economy*, 84: 937–957.

FitzGerald, J. (2006), 'Lessons From 20 Years of Cohesion', in Mundschenk, S., Stierle, M.H., Stierle-von Schultz, U. and Traistaru, I. (Eds.), *Competitiveness and Growth in Europe: Lessons and Policy Implications for the Lisbon Strategy*, Edward Elgar, Chaltenham, 66–100.

Flockton, C. (1998), 'Germany's Long-running Fiscal Strains: Unification Costs or Unsustainability of Welfare State Arrangements?', *Debatte*, 6(1), 79–93.

Glyn, A. (1995), 'Social Democracy and Full Employment', *New Left Review*, 211: 31–55.

Hantrais, L. (2007), *Social Policy in the European Union*, Palgrave, Basingstoke, third edition.

Hemerijck, A. and Ferrera, M. (2004), 'Welfare Reform in the Shadow of EMU', in Martin, A. and Ross, G. (Eds.), *Euros and Europeans: Monetary Integration and the European Model of Society*, Cambridge University Press, Cambridge, 248–277.

Heyes, J. (2013), 'Flexicurity in Crisis: European Labour Market Policies in a Time of Austerity', *European Journal of Industrial Relations*, 19(1): 71–86.

Hodge, S. and Howe, J. (1999), 'Can the European Social Model Survive?', *European Urban and Regional Studies*, 6(2): 178–184.

Hoffmann, J. (2002), 'Beyond the Myth: International Solidarity as a Challenge to Trade Unions in the Age of Globalisation and Europeanisation', in Hoffmann, J. (Ed.), *The Solidarity Dilemma*, ETUI, Brussels, 119–144.

Holland, S. (1995), 'Squaring the Circle? The Maastricht Convergence Criteria, Cohesion and Employment', in Coates, K. and Holland, S. (Eds.), *Full Employment for Europe*, Spokesman, Nottingham, 90–122.

Holmlund, B. (1988), 'Arbetsmarknadspolitik och lönebildning' [Labour Market Policy and Wage Formation], in Björklund, A. (Ed.), *90-talets arbetsmarknad* [The Labour Market in the 1990s], Allmänna förlaget, Stockholm.

Horn, G.A. and Zwiener, R. (1992), 'Wage Regimes in a United Europe', in Barrell, R. and Whitley, J. (Eds.), *Macroeconomic Policy Co-Ordination in Europe*, Sage, London, 83–101.

Hunt, J. (2006), *The Economics of German Reunification*. Available via: www.rci.rutgers.edu/~jah357/Hunt/Transition_files/german_unification.pdf.

Hutton, W. (1994), *The State We're In*, Cape, London.

Hyman, R. (2005), 'Trade Unions and the Politics of the European Social Model', *Economic and Industrial Democracy*, 26(1): 9–40.

ILO [International Labour Organisation] (1995), *From Protection to Destitution*, International Labour Organisation, Geneva.

Issing, O. (2000), 'Europe, Common Money – Political Union?', *Economic Affairs*, March: 33–39.

Iversen, T. (1999), *Contested Economic Institutions: The Politics of Macroeconomics and Wage Bargaining in Advanced Democracies*, Cambridge University Press, Cambridge.

Jackman, R., Pissarides, C. and Savouri, S. (1990), 'Labour Market Policies and Unemployment in the OECD', *Economic Policy*, 5(2): 449–490.

Keller, B. and Sorries, B. (1997), 'The New Social Dialogue: Procedural Structuring, First Results and Perspectives', *Industrial Relations Journal (European Annual Review)*, 77–98.

Keynes, J.M. (1936), *The General Theory of Employment, Interest and Money*, Macmillan, London, 1973 edition.

Korpi, W. (1985), 'Economic Growth and the Welfare System: Leaky Bucket or Irrigation System?', *European Sociological Review*, 1: 97–118.

Korpi, W. (1996), 'Eurosclerosis and the Sclerosis of Objectivity: On the Role of Values Among Economic Policy Experts', *Economic Journal*, 106(439): 1727–1746.

Kregel, J., Matzner, E. and Grabher, G. (1992), *Market Shock: An Agenda for Economic and Social Reconstruction of Central and Eastern Europe*, University of Michigan Press, Ann Arbor, MI.

Lawrence, R. and Schultz, C. (Eds.) (1987), *Barriers to European Growth: A Transatlantic View*, Brookings Institution, Washington, DC.

Leibfried, S. (1994), 'The Social Dimension of the European Union: En Route to Positively Joint Sovereignty?', *Journal of European Social Policy*, 4(4): 239–262.

Leibfried, S. and Pierson, P. (1995), 'The Dynamics of Social Policy Integration', in Leibfried, S. and Pierson, P. (Eds.), *Fragmented Social Policy: The European Community's Social Dimension in Comparative Perspective*, Brookings Institution, Washington, DC.

Lindbeck, A., Molander, P., Persson, T., Petersson, O., Sandmo, A., Swedenborg, B. and Thygesen, N. (1994), *Turning Sweden Around*, MIT Press, London.

Lumley, R. (1996), 'Labour Markets and Employment Relations in Transition: The Case of German Unification', *Employee Relations*, 17(1): 24–37.

Martin, A. and Ross, G. (1999), 'In the Line of Fire: The Europeanization of Labor Representation', in Martin, A. and Ross, G. (Eds.), *The Brave New World of European Labor: European Trade Unions at the Millennium*, Berghahn Books, Oxford, 312–367.

Martin, J.P. and Scarpetta, S. (2012), 'Setting It Right: Employment Protection, Labour Reallocation and Productivity', *De Economist*, 160(2): 89–116.

Mathers, A. (2007), *Struggling for a Social Europe*, Ashgate, Aldershot.

McNamara, K. (1998), *The Currency of Ideas: Monetary Politics in the European Union*, Cornell University Press, Ithaca, NY.

Meidner, R. (1983), 'Strategy for Full Employment', Paper presented to the *Public Services International Symposium on the Public Service*, 9–11 September, Stockholm.

Melitz, J. (1997), 'The Evidence About the Costs and Benefits of EMU', *Swedish Economic Policy Review*, 4: 359–410.

Moss, B.H. (2005), 'The EU as a Neo-Liberal Construction', in Moss, B.H. (Ed.), *Monetary Union in Crisis: The European Union as a Neo-Liberal Construction*, Palgrave, Basingstoke, 1–25.

OECD (2010), *OECD Employment Outlook 2010: Moving Beyond the Jobs Crisis*, OECD Publishing, Paris. Available via: http://dx.doi.org/10.1787/empl_outlook-2010-en.

OECD (2013), 'Protecting Jobs, Enhancing Flexibility: A New Look at Employment Protection Legislation', *OECD Outlook 2013*, OECD Publishing, Paris. Available via: http://dx.doi.org/10.1787/empl_outlook-2013-6-en.

Peters, T. (1995), 'European Monetary Union and Labour Markets: What to Expect', *International Labour Review*, 134(3): 315–332.

Pissarides, C. (1997), 'The Need for Labour Market Flexibility in European Economic and Monetary Union', *Swedish Economic Policy Review*, 4(2): 513–546.

Rhodes, M. (1992), 'The Future of the Social Dimension: Labour Market Regulation in Post-1992 Europe', *Journal of Common Market Studies*, 30(1): 23–51.

Ross, G. and Martin, A. (1999), 'European Unions Face the Millennium', in Martin, A. and Ross, G. (Eds.), *The Brave New World of European Labor*, Barghahn Books, Oxford, 1–25.

Rowthorn, R.E. (1995), 'Capital Formation and Unemployment', *Oxford Review of Economic Policy*, 11(1): 26–39.

Rowthorn, R.E. and Glyn, A. (1990), 'The Diversity of Unemployment Experience Since 1973', in Marglin, S. and Schor, J. (Eds.), *The Golden Age of Capitalism: Reinterpreting the Postwar Experience*, Clarendon, Oxford, 187–217.

Schettkat, R. (2003), 'Are Institutional Rigidities at the Root of European Unemployment?', *Cambridge Journal of Economics*, 27(6): 771–787.

Sinn, G. and Sinn, H.-W. (1992), *Jumpstart: The Economic Unification of Germany*, MIT Press, Cambridge, MA.

Stiglitz, J.A. (2016), *The Euro and Its Threat to the Future of Europe*, Allen Lane, London.

Strange, G. (1997), 'The British Labour Movement and Economic and Monetary Union in Europe', *Capital and Class*, 63: 13–24.

Streeck, W. (1992), *Social Institutions and Economic Performance: Studies of Industrial Relations in Advanced Capitalist Economies*, Sage, London.

Swenson, P. (1989), *Fair Shares: Unions, Pay and Politics in Sweden and West Germany*, Cornell University Press, Ithaca, USA.

Teague, P. (1997), 'Lean Production and the German Model', *German Politics*, 6(2): 76–94.

Teague, P. (1998), 'Monetary Union and Social Europe', *Journal of European Social Policy*, 8(2): 117–139.

Turner, L. (1996), 'The Europeanisation of Labour: Structure Before Action', *European Journal of Industrial Relations*, 2(3): 325–344.

Vaughan-Whitehead, D.C. (2003), *EU Enlargement Versus Social Europe? The Uncertain Future of the European Social Model*, Edward Elgar, Cheltenham.

Watson, M. (2006), 'The European Social Model: Between a Rock and a Hard Place?', in Whyman, P.B., Baimbridge, M. and Burkitt, B. (Eds.), *Implications of the Euro: A Critical Perspective From the Left*, Routledge, London, 145–154.

Whyman, P.B. (2001), 'Can Opposites Attract? Monetary Union and the Social Market', *Contemporary Politics*, 7(2): 113–128.

Whyman, P.B. (2002), 'British Trade Unions and EMU', *Industrial Relations*, 41(3): 467–476.

Whyman, P.B. (2003), *Sweden and the 'Third Way': A Macroeconomic Evaluation*, Ashgate, Aldershot.

Whyman, P.B. (2006), *Third Way Economics*, Palgrave, Basingstoke.

Whyman, P.B. (2007), 'The European Social Model and EMU', in Baimbridge, M. and Whyman, P. (Eds.), *Britain, the Euro and Beyond*, Ashgate, Aldershot.

Whyman, P.B., Baimbridge, M. and Mullen, A. (2012), *The Political Economy of the European Social Model*, Routledge, Abingdon.

Whyman, P.B. and Petrescu, A.I. (2014), 'Partnership, Flexible Workplace Practices and the Realisation of Mutual Gains: Evidence From the British WERS Dataset', *International Journal of Human Resource Management*, 25(6): 821–851.

Wilkinson, R. and Pickett, K. (2009), *The Spirit Level: Why More Equal Societies Almost Always Do Better*, Allen Lane, London.

Conclusion

The purpose of this book is to outline the flaws and fundamental weaknesses inherent within the current neo-liberal model of EMU, and to contrast this with a post-Keynesian approach to economic and currency union. The ICU alternative would achieve most of the objectives of the current system, in that it promotes closer economic integration between participants. However, the difference is that it would do so by creating a supportive economic infrastructure within which participant economies could better pursue goals of full employment and economic growth, thereby improving the lives of all of its citizens. The ICU structure would be sufficiently flexible to prevent the creation and persistence of imbalances within the union, which would eventually fracture the economic arrangement much as occurred during previous attempts at fixed and single currency arrangements. However, it would be sufficiently rigorous as to promote systematic rebalancing, involving both surplus and deficit nations, without imposing all of the costs of adjustment upon the latter.

The original ICU proposal was ahead of its time, and this perhaps explains why it was overlooked in favour of the eventual Bretton Woods arrangement as the basis for the post-Second World War international monetary architecture. Yet, the motivations behind its creation would appear tailor-made for the Eurozone. Keynes devised the ICU as a means of creating a currency arrangement (or union) that would not have a built in tendency towards deflation and under-employment, but would rather create conditions conducive to its participant economies pursuing full employment and growth. In so doing, it would provide fertile ground for the creation of a fully fledged ESM, of the type that many in the EU advocate for, but which appears to be at odds with the requirements and discipline imposed by the neo-liberal form of EMU. However, if a particular form of economic model appears outdated and is in the way of Europe realising its goals, then there is a strong case for its replacement with a system that is more compatible.

The potential replacement of the current neo-liberal model of EMU is, moreover, aided by the existence of certain institutional forms, such as the ECB, that are accepted by participants to perform functions necessary for the stabilisation of the current single currency system. Once properly reformed, and provided with a new set of objectives to pursue, there is no reason why the K-ECB could not form the fulcrum of an ICU common currency union.

The EU has a second advantage, in that the 'European project' is intended to operate according to principles of solidarity between participating member states. This has not always been adhered to very closely in practice. Indeed, the behaviour of the 'troika' during the Eurozone crisis would have severely strained such notions of mutual assistance between member states. Nevertheless, the fact that EMU rests upon such a potentially powerful foundation 'myth' should make it easier to gain acceptance from those member states currently running large trade surpluses that their best interests, along with those of their neighbours, lie in symmetrical solutions to economic problems. Rather than all of the costs of adjustment being loaded upon economies already struggling with competitiveness issues, solidarity would suggest that *all* member states should share in any necessary adjustment, and equally they should all share in the benefits arising from a better functioning system in the future.

The ICU proposal offers this potential. If those member states running surpluses do indeed believe in the concept of European solidarity, they should be more likely to perceive the advantages in adopting the Keynesian approach, as it would promote greater prosperity for all participants and provide a more stable basis for any future moves towards deeper economic integration.

This is not to suggest that the ICU would prove to be a panacea for all economic problems facing the European economy. However, it has the potential to provide a superior alternative to the present solutions (Arestis, 1999: 1). It would be possible, for example, for shifts in international competitiveness to be swiftly dealt with, in the absence of painful adjustment that stretched internal solidarity. It would also encourage the Eurozone economy to operate closer to full employment, with faster rates of economic growth, which would mark a significant improvement over achievements since the advent of the Euro. Moreover, the creation of a more flexible system, in which the objectives of employment and economic prosperity dominate over financial considerations, might encourage more nations to participate in the system. Thus, perhaps it might be time for EU economists and policymakers to dust off their copies of the Keynes Plan and familiarise themselves with the contents – it might prove instructive.

Bibliography

Arestis, P. (1999), 'The Independent European Central Bank: Keynesian Alternatives', *Jerome Levy Economics Institute Working Paper* No. 274. Available via: https://papers.ssrn.com/sol3/papers.cfm?abstract_id=174852.

Index

For Product Safety Concerns and Information please contact our EU
representative GPSR@taylorandfrancis.com
Taylor & Francis Verlag GmbH, Kaufingerstraße 24, 80331 München, Germany

www.ingramcontent.com/pod-product-compliance
Ingram Content Group UK Ltd.
Pitfield, Milton Keynes, MK11 3LW, UK
UKHW020945180425
457613UK00019B/538